canapés

canapés

DK LONDON
Senior Editor Bob Bridle
Senior Art Editor Lucy Parissi
Project Editor Martha Burley
Cookery Editor Kathy Steer
Managing Editor Dawn Henderson
Managing Art Editor Christine Keilty
Senior Jacket Creative Nicola Powling
Jacket Design Assistant Rosie Levine
Production Editors Luke Palmer
Senior Production Editor Tony Phipps
Senior Production Controller Jen Lockwood

DK INDIA
Project Editor Manasvi Vohra
Senior Editor Nidhilekha Mathur
Senior Art Editor Balwant Singh
Assistant Editor Aditi Batra
Managing Editor Glenda Fernandes
Managing Art Editor Navidita Thapa
CTS/DTP Manager Sunil Sharma
Senior DTP Designer Tarun Sharma
DTP Designer Anurag Trivedi

PHOTOGRAPHY
William Reavell and Ian O'Leary

First published in Great Britain in 2012 by
Dorling Kindersley Limited
80 Strand, London WC2R 0RL
Penguin Group (UK)

Copyright © 2012 Dorling Kindersley Limited

2 4 6 8 10 9 7 5 3
004-182924-Oct/2012

A CIP catalogue record for this book is available from the
British Library.
ISBN 978-1-4093-7585-2

Colour reproduction by Opus Multimedia Services, India
Printed and bound in South China

Discover more at
www.dk.com

contents

Introduction

Since Eric Treuille and I wrote the first canapé book in 1998, brilliantly assisted and aided by Rosie Kindersley, I have wanted to add to its marvellous collection of mouth-watering mini meals. I travel through my culinary life looking at, tasting, and thinking of canapés – what will work, what will minimize, and what is practical? Turning starters, main courses, and even desserts into one mouthful creates a sense of fun and delight that all good party food should.

As a professional cook who runs a catering business and prepares and serves thousands of canapés every year, I am always realistic about making the recipe work, not only for the cook but also for the guest. There is no point suggesting and serving a canapé that has so many stages it takes forever to make. By the time it is served it may be cold, soggy, or may have even collapsed, and then the guests may have an embarrassing time trying to work out how to eat it! I believe in serving fresh, vibrant food with great flavours that have not been messed around with.

Serving canapés to your guests is a fun way of showing off – not only your organizational skills, but your knowledge of cooking and of pairing up assorted flavours, including different influences from other cuisines. For example, it is the one time you can mix a little Asian and French together, as long as you make some considerations for taste, texture, and presentation when choosing your menu.

Serving canapés at a party is a practical way of feeding a crowd, especially if you are limited in space, time, and equipment. It is a relief not to have to be counting out and washing up endless plates, knives, and forks. All your guests require is a drink, a cocktail napkin, and a warm welcome.

All these recipes include lots of tips and advice on how to get ahead and how to make and store the food in advance, so you can manage your time and also enjoy entertaining as much as your guests will love the treats that you present to them. Obviously throwing a canapé party takes some planning even for the most experienced of cooks and hosts and so I have included *Planning your party* with advice on what to serve as well as *Menu Planners*, which will set you straight on your way to success.

We hope this book will give you the confidence to enjoy hosting a canapé party for many different occasions including birthdays, work parties, family reunions, festive fun, weddings, christenings, or just a get-together with friends. Explore our recipes, add your own ideas and favoured herbs and spices and make this book a well-thumbed, well-loved, and well-used kitchen staple.

Start planning, start cooking, start eating, and enjoy.

Victoria Blashford-Snell

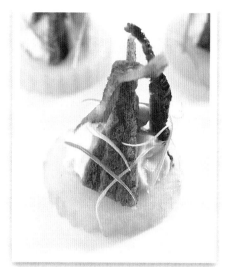

PLANNING YOUR PARTY

Getting started

Being organized is the secret to hosting a successful party. Start by working out the logistics before planning your canapé menu.

Who is coming to the party?

Assessing your guest list is a great place to kick off your party plan. At informal get-togethers family and friends are more than happy to tuck in to party food such as dippers with dips and basic canapés, but on occasion your menu will need to be carefully tailored to your guests. Menu choices should be relevant to their age range and how familiar they are with each other. Often parties include a mix of age groups, so try to consider this and provide something for all tastes and expectations.

Check the guest list for anyone who may be vegetarian or has special dietary requirements – whether medical or religious – and design your menu accordingly. Combining a selection of hot and cold canapés, a couple of classic recipes, as well as something more adventurous will help you to create a varied menu for guests with individual tastes.

How much space do you have?

Account for the amount of space you will have available to entertain your guests. If it is limited, do not plan to serve canapés on large platters, which are hard to pass around among a crowd of clustered guests. If you place platters on a serving table in a crowded room it can be difficult for guests to help themselves. Choose a delicious, simple-to-eat selection of canapés to hand around, allowing you to circulate and welcome your guests.

When planning your party, consider the space you have to prepare your canapés in, too. It would be disastrous to find that the guests are arriving any minute and you have trays of unfinished canapés spread all over the house. Take into consideration how big your oven is, and try not to choose canapé recipes that require different oven temperatures. If you have one oven, do you need a grill? Do you need to deep-fry? Where will you do it?

Generous fridge space will be a real help, but it may be limited due to drink supply, so at least one

BE SPACE AWARE Placing canapés on a serving table may make them difficult to reach. Instead, use platters, which can be easily passed around.

> *Take practical considerations into account when working on menu choices – try to avoid last-minute assembling and make sure some canapés can be made in advance.* **"**

BE PREPARED Place fresh herbs and other ingredients that are needed for garnishing in little bowls ready for use.

week before the party, try to use up the things that have been there for months. This process will may also prompt you to compile a shopping list.

Use your larder or cupboards to store trays of food, helping to keep your work surfaces free for last-minute garnishing and plating up of hot food.

If you have a room near to the kitchen that is not needed for the party, pop up a table and use it as extra space for food and drink storage.

Guests often gather in the kitchen and want to talk, but it can be tricky working efficiently around them. Plan to be as organized as possible with chopped herbs and spices for garnishing in separate bowls, ready for use. It is very useful to have a clear sink and surfaces during the party, so allow 20 minutes to clean up before the final stages of canapé presentation and serving start.

FUN AND DELICIOUS If children are on your guest list, choose fun recipes or novelty presentation options to keep them entertained.

Plan your time

Try to keep your party timetable in mind at all times during preparation. If you are in a rush it is doubtful that the finished result will be as good as intended. Plan well and prepare ahead where possible. Many canapé bases can be made well in advance and stored, so choose some of those to go on your menu.

Take practical considerations into account when working on menu choices – try to avoid lots of last-minute assembling and make sure that some canapés can be fully prepared ahead.

After you have chosen your menu, make a shopping list. This can be done well in advance and, if it helps, you can choose to order any necessary ingredients online and have them delivered. Try making a time plan stating when you will prepare things. This is very useful and should help you to remember everything.

CHECKLIST

Find out who's coming and whether any guests have allergies or intolerances

*

Create a timetable working up to the party

*

Make space in the fridge and on work surfaces

*

Think about what you can do to get ahead

What shall I serve?

Choose a simple, well-balanced menu that includes a variety of textures, colours, and flavours, and don't forget about the presentation.

Selecting your recipes

Now for the fun part: getting creative with your menu! Many factors will affect your choice – think about the current season, the time of party, and the colours, flavours, and textures of your canapés. Avoid repeating flavours and ingredients too much.

Refer to the seasons for inspiration, as it is always a delight to serve a special seasonal treat. Seasonal ingredients are also reasonably priced and widely available. When sourcing your ingredients, try to buy the best possible quality as it makes a huge difference to the finished canapé.

FLAVOUR ENHANCERS As most canapés are single mouthfuls, choose strong flavours, such as chilli, soy sauce, and ginger.

Try not to include too many new recipes in your menu and always make sure you have tried-and-tested favourites. Avoid choosing a lot of recipes that take a long time to make. If possible, test out new recipes before the party. Sometimes it suits to serve a simple menu if your time or budget is tight – your canapés can still be exquisite.

Balancing the menu

Choose a good combination of poultry, fish, seafood, red meat, and vegetables. If you are serving hot food, do not have too many fried canapés (although they are often popular!), or too many seared or baked ones. With cold canapés, choose some gluten-free ones and a few vegetarian choices. It may sound elaborate, but armed with the variety of canapés in this book you'll have plenty to choose from.

Most of your canapés should be a single bite, so it is important to get the flavours right. Taste as you cook, as you only have one chance to impress with a canapé, unlike a plate of food where one can enjoy the flavours developing with each mouthful. Canapé recipes often use strong flavours, and citrus zests, juices, chilli, soy sauce, and salt and pepper are often used to enhance the flavours.

All in the presentation

Creating interesting plates of food can be great fun. If theming your menu around your food

" Refer to the seasons for inspiration. It can be a real delight to serve a special seasonal treat, such as asparagus or mussels."

choices or the occasion, you could garnish your canapés with herbs, zests, and spices, but do avoid anything on top of the food that is not edible.

CREATIVE PRESENTATION Textured materials such as banana leaves or coarse sea salt can jazz up plain platters. Fresh herb garnishes add colour and accents of flavour.

Practice can make perfect when it comes to creating your canapés. Do not overfill the bases or spoons as this can make them go soggy, topple over, or difficult to eat. Try not be a miser with your fillings either! Being careful with presentation gets good results. Taste one canapé first, before serving, to check you are happy them.

When decorating your serving plates, you could use fresh sturdy flowers and clusters of wild herbs. Nightlight candles placed in little pots are also very effective, as are banana leaves, bamboo mats, slates, smooth wooden boards, patterned or plain white china plates, and clear or brightly coloured glass plates. Look out for different serving dishes on your travels, but make sure they have a flat surface as plates and platters that are slightly indented are difficult to use – the canapés are prone to falling over.

Serving crudités with dips, skewered foods, fried morsels, and crisp breads can be messy, so make sure the dip bowl is kept clean during your party. Use a clean bowl each time you need to refill, rather than just refilling the bowl. Provide little dipping bowls, which don't need to match, and always make sure you are armed with little cocktail napkins and another bowl to place used cocktail sticks in. With these expert tips and tricks, you will be able to enjoy your party and the inevitable praise from contented guests.

When assembling your canapés make sure there is enough of the topping or filling, but don't add too much, or they will be inelegant and tricky to eat.

Do the maths

Getting the quantities right for your canapés is all-important, but can prove tricky. Help is at hand for creating your perfect party menu.

When is the party?

Is it a midday party or an evening event? Will your guests have travelled far and is a meal going to be served later? You may be serving during a sporting event, giving guests heartier appetites. People tend to eat more in colder weather and enjoy lighter food in the warmer months – there are summer and winter planners on the following pages to help you.

Multiplying recipe quantities

You may find that you need to double or triple your quantities for larger parties. Doubling a recipe is straightforward and works well, but once you start tripling, ingredients and flavours can react differently. Liquid quantities require attention – it is best not to add all the liquid ingredients immediately. When multiplying dipping sauces, you may not require three times the quantity, even if you do need to triple the rest of the recipe. For example, a fish cake recipe would need tripled fish, potato, and herb quantities, but not lemon juice – or seasoning quantities. Instead, double the amounts, taste, and add more as required.

If in doubt...

When catering for larger numbers, allow more canapés, as although some guests may not turn up, others may bring another guest. Some guests will eat more than others, but do try to reach everyone. Try to avoid those guests who deliberately hang around at the kitchen door hoping to intercept plates of canapés before they reach the other guests!

HOW MANY CANAPÉS SHOULD I SERVE?

TYPE OF PARTY

Pre-lunch or dinner drinks
5 pieces per guest
Choose 3–4 different canapés

First course canapés
6 pieces per guest
Choose 5 different canapés

Drinks party (approx 2½ hrs)
10 pieces per guest
Choose 7–10 different canapés

Canapé-only evening party
14 pieces per guest
Choose 8–14 different canapés

All-day celebration
12–14 pieces per guest
Choose 8–10 savoury canapés and
2–4 sweet canapés

" *When catering for larger numbers, allow slightly more canapés, as although some guests may not turn up, others may bring another guest.* "

TAKE CARE Liquid quantities and strong flavours such as soy sauce and Thai fish sauce require particular attention when you are multiplying quantities in recipes.

Below are quantity guidelines for different types of party. Create a menu with both hot and cold recipes for your party, using these examples as inspiration. Note the mixture of bases and different techniques in each menu. If you are concerned about timing, it may be best to attempt fewer recipes, doubling up on the easiest recipe.

COLD CANAPÉ IDEAS

Tomato concasse with crème fraîche and chive croustades p120 • Green olive and basil tapenade oatcakes p46 (pictured)

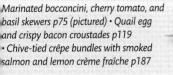

Marinated bocconcini, cherry tomato, and basil skewers p75 (pictured) • Quail egg and crispy bacon croustades p119 • Chive-tied crêpe bundles with smoked salmon and lemon crème fraîche p187

Bresaola wrapped figs with rocket and Parmesan skewers p75 • Parmesan shortbread with beetroot pesto p42 (pictured) • Potato rösti with crème fraîche, caviar, and dill p147

Mini poppadoms with creamy chicken tikka p49 • Filo tartlets with spicy coriander prawns p168 (pictured) • Goat's cheese and roasted cherry tomato crostini p110 • Fresh crab with avocado and lemon salad spoons p54

Chicken Caesar salad wraps p188 • Smoked salmon and citrus-chive cream sandwiches p203 • Rare roast beef with horseradish cream sandwiches p202 (pictured) • Lemon mascarpone with mint and raspberry oatcakes p47 • Muscovado and fig mini meringues p211

HOT CANAPÉ IDEAS

Aubergine and pine nut fritters with roast tomato sauce p161 (pictured) • Gingered chicken cakes with coriander-lime mayonnaise p154

Thai chicken and lemongrass sticks with sweet cucumber dipping sauce p76 • Spiced vegetable pakoras with tomato and ginger dipping sauce p153 (pictured)

Fragrant coconut prawn spoons p54 (pictured) • Aubergine and pine nut pizzette p137 • Cumin-scented kofte brochettes with minted yogurt dip p82 • Mini devilled crab cakes with tomato remoulade p160

Eggs Benedict p60 (pictured) • Clams with ginger and lime butter p51 • Prosciutto-wrapped scallop brochettes with sauce béarnaise p64 • Crispy courgette goujons with parsley, lemon, and Parmesan p155

Lamb fillet with pomegranate and mint skewers p74 (pictured) • Mini croque monsieur p201 • Honey sesame glazed cocktail sausages p101 • Smoked haddock and parsley cakes p158 • Spiced squash samosas with yogurt-harissa dip p180

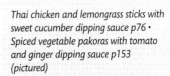

Don't forget the drinks

The canapés are sure to impress, but what about the drinks? Here are some useful ideas about what to serve and how much you'll need.

What to serve

Deciding what drinks to serve depends a lot on the occasion and your budget. First of all, soft drinks are essential. Cool water is necessary – make sure it is available to guests at all times.

Some of your guests may be tee-totallers or designated drivers, so provide an interesting soft drink for them. When buying ready-made soft drinks, avoid the cheaper brands, as they tend to be packed full of artificial sweeteners, which are sticky, overly sugary, and unpleasant. Choose from lemonade, limeade, ginger beer, cranberry, apple, or other delicious fresh juices. An all-time favourite is elderflower cordial, which you can mix 50/50 with ginger beer, adding ice and mint leaves. Home-made or good-quality soft drinks with lots of ice and sparkling water are popular, especially when garnished with mint leaves, slices of cucumber, or citrus wedges. Fruit can create a splash of colour and taste for many drinks – try adding pretty slices of strawberry and kiwi fruit. To keep cool, you could pop frozen fruits into the drinks before serving, or place a berry in an ice-cube tray, fill up with cold water and freeze to make berry ice cubes.

Toasting to the occasion

The kinds of alcoholic drinks you may offer depend on your budget – sparkling wines such as Champagne or Prosecco will always create a buzz of excitement. Choose your wine to match flavour pairings in the food, and remember that spritzers – chilled white wine mixed 50/50 with sparkling mineral water – are refreshing, popular, and can help your supply last the evening. Beer and cider could also be suitable on a hot day.

Cocktails are a fun and delicious choice. Don't make them too strong, so that your party lasts! Provide a choice of one or two non-alcoholic cocktails alongside the boozy ones.

Chilling your drinks

Allow time to chill your drinks. If you are chilling drinks in a fridge, you can place them in several days in advance, or, at the least, 4 hours before

THINK AHEAD Make sure you have enough suitable glasses for your party; you may need to borrow or hire them.

Cocktails are a fun and popular choice. Don't make them too strong, so that your party lasts! Provide some non-alcoholic cocktails alongside the boozy ones. **"**

REFRESHING CHOICES Be sure to provide at least two different types of soft drinks and plenty of water at your party.

the party. But if you don't have the luxury of space, then use ice. You will need to place the bottles in a large (waterproof) chilling bin and cover with ice. Do not add water, as this could ruin the labels.The bottles can safely sit in the ice for up to 6 hours – 3 hours before the party for chilling, and then 3 hours during the party – but top up with ice when it starts to melt. Keep the chilling bins in the shade or under a table.

HOW MUCH SHOULD I SERVE?

Here are suggestions for drinks you could offer at a two-hour party. You won't need all five options – they are all listed to give an idea of quantity – but an ideal would be to mix and match two or three of them, choosing at least one non-alcoholic option. Consider contacting a local supplier who can offer tastings and delivery, and is happy to take returns – perfect for any unopened bottles of wine.

HOW MUCH PER PERSON	WHAT YOU'LL NEED
½ a bottle of sparkling wine	Flutes or saucers, ice buckets
½ a bottle of wine	Red wine glasses and white wine glasses
3 cocktails or non-alcoholic cocktails	Martini glasses or tall glasses, large pitchers
½ litre of soft drinks or water	Tall tumblers or coloured glasses, large pitchers
3 bottles of beer or cider	Tall tumblers

Menu planner **Summer party**

Keep flavours cool and light in the summer. These menus show that even on a warm day, both hot and cold recipes are recommended.

MENU 1

Marinated boccocini with cherry tomatoes and basil p75

***

Crispy courgette goujons with parsley, lemon, and Parmesan p155

***

Chilled pea and avocado soup shot p102

***

Classic prawn cocktail spoons p55

***

Devilled crab cakes with tomato remoulade p160

***

Lamb fillet with pomegranate and mint skewers p74

MENU 2

Seared sesame tuna with wasabi-avocado on tortilla crisps p124

***

Parmesan shortbreads with parsley pesto and goat's cheese p40

***

Sun-blushed tomato pesto crostini p110

***

Thai chicken and lemongrass sticks with sweet cucumber dipping sauce p76

***

Asian pork balls with chilli-lime dipping sauce p85

***

Classic fish goujons p99

Classic prawn cocktail spoons

Lamb fillet with pomegranate and mint skewers

Classic fish goujons

" Fresh-tasting ingredients such as juicy tomato, zingy citrus fruit, and delicate seafood are wonderful at this time of year. Chicken skewers and chilli marinades hint at flavours of the barbecue, complemented by cooling avocado salads. "

MENU 3

Courgette and saffron bruschetta p112

***

Mini devilled crab cakes with tomato remoulade p160

***

Goat's cheese and caramelized red onion quesadillas with salsa cruda p129

***

Chilled spiced chickpea soup cups with avocado salsa p105

***

Spicy satay sticks p81

***

Filo tartlets with spicy coriander prawns p168

MENU 4

Marinated king prawns wrapped in mangetout skewers p74

***

Fresh crab with avocado and lemon salad spoons p54

***

Goat's cheese and roasted cherry tomato crostini p110

***

Aubergine and pine nut fritters with roast tomato sauce p161

***

Sesame prawn toasts p156

***

Lime-marinated chicken skewers with avocado crème dip p80

Courgette and saffron bruschetta

Goat's cheese and roasted cherry tomato crostini

Fresh crab with avocado and lemon salad spoons

Menu planner **Winter party**

These menus with mostly warm canapés are wholly fulfilling in the cooler months. Dashes of chilli will help to warm the mood!

MENU 1

Stuffed medjool dates wrapped in prosciutto skewers p74

***

Smoked eel with horseradish and beetroot oatcakes p47

***

Hoisin-chilli duck wraps p189

***

Gratinated mussels with parsley and Parmesan crumbs p52

***

Parmesan shortbreads with tapenade p41

***

Spiced squash samosas with yogurt-harissa dip p180

MENU 2

Eggs Benedict p60

***

Smoked haddock and parsley cakes p158

***

Asian pork balls with chilli-lime dipping sauce p85

***

Bresaola wrapped figs with rocket and Parmesan skewers p75

***

Parmesan shortbreads with beetroot pesto p42

***

Filo tartlets with smoked chicken, black olives, and parsley pesto p169

Spiced squash samosas with yogurt-harissa dip

Parmesan shortbreads with beetroot pesto

Eggs Benedict

Wintry weather encourages us to create substantial menus with heavier textures and warm, creamy flavours. Canapés can be light in nature, so choose filling and hearty basics such as beetroot, duck, and beef to keep appetites at bay.

MENU 3

Mini Scotch eggs p53

***

Seared scallops, pea purée, and crisp pancetta spoons p55

***

Classic cheese quesadilla with green chilli, coriander, and avocado salsa p130

***

Goat's cheese and chilli jam oatcakes p47

***

Smoked trout and red pepper cream wraps p188

***

Filo tartlets with Asian beef salad p170

MENU 4

Shredded spiced pork quesadilla with sour cream p128

***

Beetroot rösti with smoked trout and horseradish mousse p146

***

Mushroom and chive hollandaise tartlets p175

***

Quail egg and crispy bacon croustades p119

***

Sesame soy glazed beef skewers p83

***

Caramelized red onions with Manchego and figs oatcakes p46

Filo tartlets with Asian beef salad

Quail egg and crispy bacon croustades

Menu planner **Afternoon tea**

Put a spin on tradition and serve a selection of sweet and savoury canapés with a focus on indulgent taste sensations.

MENU 1

Eggs Benedict p60

***

Prawn, avocado, and bacon finger sandwiches p202

***

Chicken Caesar salad wrap p188

***

Lemon mascarpone with mint and raspberry oatcakes p47

***

Tiny Devonshire cream tea scones with raspberry conserve p215

***

Cherry and almond frangipane tartlets p212

MENU 2

Citrus prawn wraps p188

***

Rare roast beef with horseradish cream sandwiches p202

***

Cucumber and mint finger sandwiches p203

***

Muscovado and fig mini meringues p211

***

Caramelized lemon tartlets p213

***

Mini chocolate truffle cakes p216

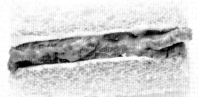

Rare roast beef with horseradish cream finger sandwiches

Tiny Devonshire cream scones with raspberry conserve

Cucumber and mint finger sandwiches

" What a treat this time of day can be for a party or celebration. Tea menus are an indulgence – pretty and sophisticated, they can be an opportunity to show flair. Wraps, finger sandwiches, and scones are traditional teatime recipes. "

MENU 3

Chicken and tarragon finger sandwiches p202

***

Smoked salmon and citrus-chive cream finger sandwiches p203

***

Pancetta and tomato with basil and almond pesto crostini p111

***

Rolled ricotta and sage crêpes with Parmesan shavings p186

***

Strawberry and pistachio mini meringues p210

***

Triple chocolate biscottini with hazelnuts p208

MENU 4

Mini Scotch eggs p53

***

Crab and watercress mayonnaise sandwiches p203

***

Rosemary mini muffins with smoked ham and peach relish p204

***

Dill pancakes with salmon caviar and lemon crème fraîche p162

***

Mini sticky orange and almond cakes p217

***

Mini chocolate truffle cakes p216

Triple chocolate biscottini with hazelnuts

Mini sticky orange and almond cakes

Menu planner **Quick and easy**

It is still easy to make delicious food, even when in a hurry. These menus are particularly simple – perfect for those impromptu guests.

MENU 1

Marinated bocconcini with cherry tomatoes and basil skewers p75

***

Marinated Mediterranean olives p37

***

Spicy party nuts p34

***

Courgette and saffron bruschetta p112

***

Herbed yogurt dip p91

***

Mini croque monsieur p201

MENU 2

Marinated king prawns with mangetout skewers p74

***

Cucumber barquettes with smoked salmon and pickled ginger p57

***

Citrus avocado purée crostini p110

***

Bresaola wrapped figs with rocket and Parmesan skewers p75

***

Sun-dried tomato and cannellini bean dip p90

Marinated Mediterranean olives

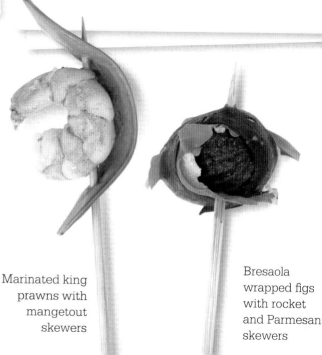

Marinated king prawns with mangetout skewers

Bresaola wrapped figs with rocket and Parmesan skewers

> " *A last-minute visit from hungry guests can provide a thrilling opportunity to practise simple canapé recipes. If you already have the ingredients then most of these dishes will take only minutes to prepare, but will look very impressive.* "

MENU 3

Honey sesame glazed cocktail sausages p101

***

Thai chicken and lemongrass sticks with sweet cucumber dipping sauce p76

***

Goat's cheese and roasted cherry tomato crostini p110

***

Cucumber cups with blue cheese mousse and crispy bacon p56

***

Vegetable dippers p97

MENU 4

Lamb fillet with pomegranate and mint skewers p74

***

Chargrilled aubergine with garlic and mint crostini p111

***

Spiced vegetable pakoras with tomato and ginger dipping sauce p153

***

Barbecued tandoori prawn sticks p67

***

Mini croque monsieur p201

***

Citrus avocado purée crostini p110

Chargrilled aubergine with garlic and mint crostini

Citrus avocado purée crostini

Vegetable dippers

Menu planner **Vegetarian feast**

A vegetarian menu should be as exciting as any other. Choose recipes with bright colours, varied textures, and contrasting flavours.

MENU 1

Rosemary flat bread with garlic, Parmesan, and olives p140

***

Sun-blushed tomato pesto crostini p110

***

Avocad, basil, and pine nut wraps p189

***

Piquant peppery hummus oatcakes p46

***

Parmesan shortbreads with tapenade (omitting the anchovies) p41

MENU 2

Sweet potato and ginger rösti with coriander pesto p148

***

Spiced vegetable pakoras with tomato and ginger dipping sauce p153

***

Chilled pea and avocado soup shots p102

***

Aubergine and pine nut pizzette p137

***

Goat's cheese and caramelized red onion quesadillas with salsa cruda p129

***

Fennel-marinated feta and olive skewers p78

Piquant peppery hummus oatcakes

Sun-blushed tomato pesto crostini

Chilled pea and avocado soup shots

" There is so much to include here – vegetables lend themselves beautifully to light bites and when combined with fragrant herbs they will even tempt meat eaters. Many vegetarian cheese varieties are available if you need them. "

MENU 3

Minted feta and pine nut filo rolls with lemon aïoli p193

***

Green olive and basil tapenade oatcakes p46

***

Tomato concasse with crème fraîche and chive croustades p120

***

Aubergine and pine nut fritters with roast tomato sauce p161

***

Rolled ricotta and sage crêpes with Parmesan shavings p186

***

Marinated bocconcini, cherry tomato, and basil skewers p75

MENU 4

Feta, olive, and rosemary tartlets p177

***

Chilled spiced chickpea soup cups with avocado salsa p105

***

Spiced squash samosas with yogurt-harissa dip p180

***

Parmesan shortbreads with beetroot pesto p42

***

Radish cups with black olive tapenade (omitting the anchovies) p59

***

Salsa romesco dip with vegetable dippers p92 and p97

Marinated bocconcini, cherry tomato, and basil skewers

Green olive and basil tapenade oatcakes

Feta, olive, and rosemary tartlets

Menu planner **World flavours**

Mix world flavours with care. Explore Asian cuisine with Menus 1 and 2, span the globe with Menu 3, or keep it continental with Menu 4.

MENU 1

Asian pork balls with chilli-lime dipping sauce p85

***

Seared beef satay spoons p55

***

Thai chicken and lemongrass sticks with sweet cucumber dipping sauce p76

***

Herbed prawn wonton crescents with a tangy lime dipping sauce p178

***

Cucumber nori sushi rolls p195

MENU 2

Fresh crab, avocado, and lemon salad spoons p54

***

Mini Peking duck pancakes with plum sauce p192

***

Salmon teriyaki skewers with ginger soy dipping sauce p70

***

Sesame soy glazed beef skewers p83

***

Crab and papaya rice paper rolls with sweet chilli dipping sauce p190

***

Spiced vegetable pakoras with tomato and ginger dipping sauce p153

Asian pork balls with chilli-lime dipping sauce

Mini Peking duck pancakes

Choose a theme for your menu that explores robust flavours from around the globe. Exotic ingredients such as ginger, coconut, and chillies in the Asian-themed menus evoke distant destinations – lovely for a conversation starter.

MENU 3

Grilled spiced pepper and chorizo wraps p189

***

Vietnamese chicken salad spoons p54

***

Moroccan-spiced swordfish brochettes p72

***

Spicy pork empanaditas with avocado relish p182

***

Fragrant coconut prawns spoons p54

***

Carrot, honey, and ginger soup cups p104

MENU 4

Prosciutto-wrapped scallop brochettes with sauce béarnaise p64

***

Eggs Benedict p60

***

Mini croque monsieur p201

***

Crispy courgette goujons with parsley, lemon, and Parmesan p155

***

Poached salmon with dill mayonnaise croustades p116

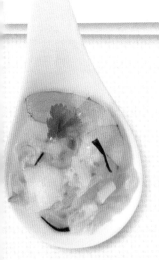

Fragrant coconut prawns spoons

Vietnamese chicken salad spoons

Eggs Benedict

THE RECIPES

little nibbles and mini mouthfuls

Spiced party nuts

Almonds toasted in herbs, spices, and rich dark sugar are a moreish snack to serve with drinks. They can be made up to a month ahead.

Makes 500ml (16fl oz)

Ingredients
250g (9oz) almonds, skinned
1 tbsp egg white,
about ½ an egg white
2 tsp dark brown sugar
2 tsp salt
½ tsp cayenne pepper
1 tbsp finely chopped rosemary

1 Preheat oven to 150°C (300°F/Gas 2).

2 Spread the almonds in a single layer on an oven tray. Roast, shaking the tray occasionally, until lightly golden, 15 minutes. Remove from oven and cool slightly.

3 Whisk the egg white until frothy and add almonds, sugar, salt, pepper, and rosemary.

4 Toss ingredients together to coat each almond well.

5 Return almonds to the oven. Roast until fragrant and golden, 20 minutes. Cool. Serve at room temperature.

GET AHEAD Make up to 3 days in advance. Cool and store in an airtight container at room temperature. Alternatively, freeze up to 1 month in advance. Defrost overnight in refrigerator. Crisp in a preheated 180°C (350°F/Gas 4) oven, 3 minutes.

COOK'S NOTE To make curried almonds omit sugar, pepper, and rosemary and replace with 1 tbsp curry powder.

Crunchy sweet and spicy pecans

The natural sweet caramel flavour of pecan works well with a little kick from the chilli. Try different dried chillies, such as sweet or even smoked ones.

Makes 500ml (16fl oz)

Ingredients
250g (9oz) pecans
1 tbsp sunflower oil
4 tbsp sugar
1 tsp salt
1½ tsp chilli powder

1 Preheat oven to 150°C (300°F/Gas 2).

2 Spread the pecans on an oven tray. Roast, shaking the tray occasionally, until nutty and toasted, 30 minutes.

3 Heat the oil in a frying pan over medium heat. Add pecans and stir to coat. Sprinkle with the sugar and salt. Cook, stirring constantly, until the sugar melts and starts to brown slightly, 5 minutes.

4 Remove from heat but continue stirring until cooled slightly.

5 Sprinkle over the chilli powder and toss to coat each nut well. Serve at room temperature.

GET AHEAD Make up to 3 days in advance. Cool and store in an airtight container at room temperature. Alternatively, freeze up to 1 month in advance. Defrost overnight in refrigerator. Crisp in a preheated 180°C (350°F/Gas 4) oven, 3 minutes.

COOK'S NOTE Use the variety of chilli powders now available at gourmet food shops to achieve slightly different flavours. Ancho chilli powder will add a hint of smoky flavour to this piquant mixture.

Twisted parsley breadsticks

These breadsticks are great party dippers and can be served with any dip. Use your favourite strong hard cheese and seasonal herbs.

Makes 35

Ingredients
1 recipe unbaked bread dough (see pp134–5)
100g (3½oz) Red Leicester or other hard orange cheese
15g (½oz) flat-leaf parsley, roughly chopped
¼ tsp cayenne pepper

1 Preheat oven to 200°C (400°F/Gas 6).

2 Roll out the dough to 15cm x 50cm (6in x 20in) rectangle. Sprinkle over the cheese, parsley, and pepper. Fold dough in half widthways.

3 Roll dough lightly to press in the filling and compress the two layers together. With a sharp knife, cut dough across into 0.5cm (¼in) wide strips. Hold ends of each strip between your fingers and twist ends in opposite directions.

4 Lay twisted strips on oiled baking sheets. Bake until crisp and golden, 15 minutes. Cool on wire rack. Serve warm or at room temperature.

....

GET AHEAD Bake up to 3 days in advance. Store in an airtight container at room temperature. Crisp in preheated 200°C (400°F/Gas 6) oven, 3 minutes.

Marinated Mediterranean olives

These work best if made a few days in advance to allow the fruits, spices, and herbs to mingle and infuse the olives.

Makes 500ml (16fl oz)

Ingredients
250g (9oz) black or green
olives or a mix of both
1 tsp fennel seeds
½ tsp cumin seeds
grated zest of ½ orange
grated zest of ½ lemon
2 finely chopped
garlic cloves
2 tsp crushed chilli flakes
1 tsp dried oregano
1 tbsp lemon juice
1 tbsp red wine vinegar
2 tbsp olive oil
1 tbsp finely chopped parsley

1 If desired, pit the olives. Toast the fennel and cumin seeds in a dry pan over low heat until aromatic, 2 minutes.

2 Combine olives, seeds, zests, garlic, chilli, oregano, lemon juice, vinegar, and oil and toss to coat each olive well. Place in an airtight container. Leave to marinate at room temperature for 8 hours.

3 Shake the container occasionally to remix the ingredients while marinating. Stir in the parsley. Serve at room temperature.

....

GET AHEAD Make up to 1 week in advance, omitting the parsley. Store in an airtight container and refrigerate. Add parsley up to 3 hours before serving.

COOK'S NOTE Warming the olives will intensify the flavours. Gently heat the marinated olives over low heat until warmed through, 5 minutes. Serve warm.

Step-by-step Parmesan shortbreads

These peppery and delectable little shortbreads make a great party classic. They stand up well to many different toppings, and can be made well ahead.

Makes 25–30
Prep 15 minutes, plus 30 minutes chilling
Cook 8–10 minutes
Freezability Freeze the dough but not once baked

Ingredients
60g (2oz) plain flour
pinch of salt
2–3 pinches cayenne pepper
45g (1½oz) chilled butter, diced
60g (2oz) Parmesan, grated

Essential equipment
5cm (2in) round cookie cutter

GET AHEAD Bake the shortbreads up to 2 weeks ahead and store in an airtight container, or freeze the unbaked shortbread shapes to bake later.

COOK'S NOTE This recipe works well made in a food processor. If you add fresh herbs or olives to the dough, this will add moisture to the mixture so will require a little more care. Chill well and when baking make sure that they are spread well apart on the baking sheet.

VARIATION Add 1 tsp chopped fresh herbs to the shortbread mixture or 1 tsp finely chopped pitted black olives. Replace the Parmesan with strong grated Cheddar.

1 Place the flour, a pinch of salt, the pepper, diced butter, and grated Parmesan cheese into a large mixing bowl.

2 Using your fingertips, gently crumble all the ingredients together until they are well combined and resemble breadcrumbs.

3 Push the ingredients together firmly to form a smooth dough. Pushing them around will help to bring the moisture out of the butter and cheese.

4 Using a rolling pin, roll out the shortbread dough on a lightly floured cool work surface until the dough is 4mm (⅛in) thick.

5 Use a cookie cutter to stamp out 25–30 shapes, gathering up and re-rolling the dough if necessary.

6 Place the pastry shapes on a baking sheet lined with greaseproof paper and chill in the refrigerator for about 30 minutes.

7 Preheat oven to 180°C (350°F/Gas 4). Remove the pastry shapes from the refrigerator and bake in the oven until slightly golden and crisp, 8–10 minutes.

8 Remove from the oven and allow to cool on a wire rack until ready to store or top. Store, place on layers of greaseproof paper in an airtight container.

Add a topping of your choice no more than 40 minutes before serving – then watch your guests devour them in minutes! Find this and other toppings on pp40–2.

Tiny Parmesan and black olive shortbreads with parsley pesto and goat's cheese

The shortbreads can be made well in advance, but top them with the pesto and goat's cheese on the day of the party.

Makes 25

Ingredients
15g (½oz) parsley
2 tbsp pine nuts
4 tbsp grated Parmesan cheese
1 garlic clove, crushed
1 tbsp olive oil
salt and freshly ground
black pepper
25 tiny Parmesan and black
olive shortbreads (see pp38–9)
100g (3½oz) fresh creamy
goat's cheese
20 parsley leaves

1 For the pesto, place the parsley, pine nuts, Parmesan, garlic, and oil in a food processor or blender; pulse to a thick paste. Add salt and pepper to taste.

2 Use a teaspoon to top shortbreads with the pesto and goat's cheese. Garnish with parsley leaves. Serve at room temperature.

GET AHEAD Make the pesto up to 3 days in advance. You can freeze the shortbreads once cut into shapes before cooking, and store when cooked for up to 1 week in an airtight container. Top shortbreads up to 2 hours before serving.

Parmesan shortbreads with tapenade

This delicious Provençal olive spread is the perfect topping for these shortbreads. Green olives would also work well.

QUICK & EASY

Makes 20

Ingredients
140g (5oz) pitted black olives
3 anchovy fillets
1 tbsp capers, rinsed and drained
1 tsp thyme
1 tsp lemon juice
1 garlic clove
2 tbsp olive oil
pinch of soft brown sugar (optional)
20 Parmesan shortbreads (see pp38–9)

1 For the tapenade, place all the ingredients in a food processor and purée until well combined.

2 Check the flavour; add a pinch of soft brown sugar, if required.

3 Use a teaspoon to top shortbreads with the tapenade.

....

GET AHEAD The tapenade can be made several days in advance. You can freeze the shortbreads once cut into shapes before cooking, and store when cooked for up to 1 week in an airtight container.

COOK'S NOTE Use good-quality olives. Serve at room temperature.

VARIATION Tapenade can also be made with good-quality pitted green olives. You can add 50g (1¾oz) drained, canned tuna to the tapenade in the food processor to make a delicious dip or canapé topping.

Parmesan shortbreads with beetroot pesto

Beetroot adds a vibrant colour and delicious earthy flavour to these cheesy shortbreads. Sprinkle the topping on carefully to ensure even distribution.

QUICK & EASY

Makes 20

Ingredients

200g (7oz) beetroot, cooked and peeled
30g (1oz) toasted pine nuts
45g (1½oz) Parmesan cheese, grated
1 garlic clove
4 tbsp olive oil
salt and freshly ground black pepper
20 Parmesan shortbreads (see pp38–9)

To garnish

15g (½oz) toasted pine nuts
10g (⅓oz) Parmesan, grated
handful of micro cress

1 For the pesto, place all the ingredients together in a food processor; pulse until a rough paste forms and the ingredients are well combined.

2 Taste to check the seasoning.

3 Use a teaspoon to top shortbreads with the pesto.

4 Garnish with the toasted pine nuts, Parmesan shavings, and micro cress. Serve at room temperature.

GET AHEAD Make the pesto 2 days in advance and store in the refrigerator.

COOK'S NOTE Dry-roast the pine nuts carefully in a frying pan until lightly coloured. This helps to enhance their flavour. It is best to roast your own. You can use bought cooked beetroot, but not the kind in vinegar.

Parmesan cheese straws

These twisted cheese straws are fun to make with all the family.
Use smoked, unsmoked, sweet, strong, or mild paprika.

Makes 40

Ingredients
250g (9oz) puff pastry
2 tsp paprika
3 tbsp grated Parmesan cheese
1 egg yolk beaten
with 1 tbsp water

1 Preheat oven to 200°C (400°F/Gas 6).

2 Roll out pastry to 15cm x 50cm (6in x 20in) triangle. Sprinkle over the paprika and 2 tbsp of the Parmesan. Spread cheese with your hands to evenly cover pastry.

3 Fold pastry in half widthways. Brush folded pastry with the beaten egg.

4 Sprinkle over remaining Parmesan. Press lightly into the pastry with hands to secure the cheese.

5 With a sharp knife, cut pastry across into 0.5cm (¼in) wide strips. Hold ends of each strip between your fingers and twist ends in opposite directions.

6 Lay twisted strips on to oiled baking sheets. Bake until crisp and golden, 7 minutes. Cool on wire racks. Serve warm or at room temperature.

....

GET AHEAD Bake up to 3 days in advance. Store in an airtight container at room temperature. Crisp in preheated 200°C (400°F/Gas 6) oven, 3 minutes.

Swiss cheese allumettes

Serve these crunchy, peppery cheese sticks with drinks on a picnic, or bag them up as a gift. To add variety, use different cheeses.

Makes 30

Ingredients
125g (4½oz) plain flour
90g (3oz) cold butter, diced
1 egg yolk
125g (4½oz) Gruyère cheese, grated
cayenne pepper
salt and freshly ground black pepper
1 egg beaten with 1 tbsp water
1 tbsp grated Parmesan cheese

Essential equipment
baking parchment

1 Place the flour, butter, egg yolk, and cheese with a pinch each of cayenne and salt and pepper in a food processor; pulse until the mixture forms a firm pastry. Turn out and knead lightly by hand until smooth.

2 Roll out pastry on a floured surface to a 0.5cm (¼in) thickness. Cut into strips about 1cm (½in) wide and 7cm (3in) long. Place 2cm (¾in) apart on baking sheets lined with baking parchment. Refrigerate until firm, 30 minutes.

3 Preheat oven to 180°C (350°F/Gas 4). Brush with beaten egg. Sprinkle with Parmesan. Bake until golden brown, 15 minutes. Cool on a wire rack. Serve warm or at room temperature, with or without dips.

GET AHEAD Make allumettes up to 2 weeks in advance. Store in an airtight container at room temperature. Alternatively, make and freeze up to 1 month in advance. Defrost and crisp for 3 minutes in preheated 200°C (400°F/Gas 6) oven.

6 ways with **oatcakes**

Oaty crisp biscuits make a reliable, versatile base for lots of delicious toppings. When well presented they can jazz up any party menu. These recipes make 20 each.

green olive and basil tapenade

Purée 100g (3½oz) pitted green olives with grated zest of ½ lemon, black pepper, 1 garlic clove, 1 tbsp olive oil, and 15g (½oz) basil leaves in a blender or food processor. Taste to check the seasoning. Mound ½ tsp of tapenade onto each oatcake with a slice of sun-blushed tomato to garnish and a strip of basil to serve. Use sun-dried tomatoes instead of sun-blushed ones, if you prefer.

caramelized red onions with Manchego and figs

Heat 3 finely sliced red onions, 1 tbsp chopped rosemary, 1 tbsp olive oil, and 20g (¾oz) butter until wilted. Add a pinch of sea salt, stir, then add 2 tbsp red wine vinegar and 1 tbsp soft brown sugar. Reduce the heat and cook for 7 minutes until caramelized. Cool. Slice 10 mini pickled figs in half. Top each oatcake with 1 tsp of onion mixture and 2 thin diagonal slices of Manchego. Garnish with ½ a fig and scatter with rosemary.

piquant peppery hummus

Purée 225g (8oz) drained canned chickpeas with 50ml (2fl oz) lemon juice, 2 garlic cloves, salt and black pepper to taste, 30ml (1fl oz) cold water, 3 mild piquant peppers, 1 seeded red chilli, 3 tbsp tahini paste, and 30ml (1fl oz) olive oil in a blender or food processor. Taste to check the seasoning. To serve, place 1 tsp of the hummus on top of each oatcake, garnish with sliced red chilli, toasted pine nuts, and/or coriander or parsley.

Know-how... how to make oatcakes

Preheat oven to 160°C (325°F/Gas 3). Combine 125g (4½oz) wholemeal flour, 150g (5½oz) oatmeal, 150g (5½oz) rolled oats, 1½ tsp baking powder, 1 tsp salt, and 1 tbsp soft brown sugar. Pour in 125g (4½oz) melted butter and mix. Add 3 tbsp water, a little at a time, kneading into a well-blended, firm dough. Halve the dough and roll out pieces on a surface dusted with oatmeal to 3mm (⅛in) thickness. Keep dusting with oatmeal. Using a 4cm (1½in) round cookie cutter, cut out 20 rounds and place on a lined baking tray. Bake for 15 minutes.

smoked eel with horseradish and beetroot

Mix 1 tbsp grated or horseradish cream into 3 tbsp of crème fraîche with salt and black pepper to taste, adding a little mustard if necessary. Cut 200g (7oz) smoked eel into small diagonal slices. Peel and grate 1 raw beetroot and mix with ½ tbsp red wine vinegar. Top each oatcake with ½ tsp of horseradish cream, a few slices of smoked eel, some marinated beetroot, a little lemon zest, black pepper, and chervil or dill.

goat's cheese and chilli jam

To make the jam, pulse 400g (14oz) tomatoes, 2 red chillies, 2 thumbs peeled fresh ginger, 2 tbsp fish sauce, and 3 peeled garlic cloves in a food processor until chunky. Place 75ml (2½fl oz) red wine vinegar and 200g (7oz) caster sugar into a saucepan and bring to a boil. Stir, then add the tomato mixture and 50g (1¾oz) raisins and simmer gently for 1 hour over low heat until thick. Cool and store the jam. Serve on oatcakes with goat's cheese and garnish with chives.

lemon mascarpone with mint and raspberries

Mix 200g (7oz) mascarpone with 2 tbsp sifted icing sugar and 2 tbsp grated lemon zest. Cut 20 large mint leaves into thin slices. Mound 1 small tsp of the lemon mascarpone mixture on top of each oatcake and top with strips of mint and whole raspberries. Decorate with a little sifted icing sugar. For a variation, replace the raspberries with a few hulled strawberries, cut in half, with grated lime zest instead of lemon.

Savoury sables

These party sables are so versatile. You can add spices, seeds, herbs, and different types of cheese. Vary the cookie cutters to suit the occasion.

Makes 40

Ingredients
250g (9oz) plain flour
175g (6oz) cold butter, diced
250g (9oz) Gruyère
cheese, grated
¼ tsp cayenne pepper
¼ tsp mustard powder
1 egg yolk beaten with
1 tbsp water

Essential equipment
6cm (2½in) star-shaped
cookie cutter
6cm (2½in) heart-shaped
cookie cutter
baking parchment

1 Place the flour, butter, cheese, pepper, and mustard powder in a food processor; pulse until the mixture forms a pastry. Add a little cold water, 1 tsp at a time, as necessary to bring the pastry together.

2 Roll out pastry on a floured surface to 0.5cm (¼in) thickness. Stamp out into decorative shapes with cookie cutters.

3 Place 2cm (¾in) apart on 2 baking sheets lined with baking parchment. Refrigerate cut pastry shapes until firm, 30 minutes.

4 Preheat oven to 180°C (350°F/Gas 4). Brush with beaten egg. Bake until golden brown, 10 minutes. Cool on a wire rack. Serve warm or at room temperature, with or without dips.

....

GET AHEAD Make sables up to 2 weeks in advance. Store in an airtight container at room temperature. Alternatively, make and freeze up to 1 month in advance. Defrost and crisp for 3 minutes in preheated 200°C (400°F/Gas 6) oven.

VARIATION
Spicy sables Place 2 tsp paprika with the other ingredients in the food processor.

Seeded sables Omit mustard powder. Place 2 tsp caraway seeds with the other ingredients in the food processor.

Herbed sables Omit mustard powder. Place 2 tsp finely chopped rosemary with the other ingredients in the food processor.

Roquefort sables Omit mustard powder and pepper. Use a combination of 125g (4½oz) crumbled Roquefort cheese and 125g (4½oz) grated Gruyère cheese.

Mini poppadoms with creamy chicken tikka

The spiced yogurt marinade tenderizes and infuses the chicken, which is then grilled and served on this traditional crisp base.

Makes 30

Ingredients
30 mini poppadoms
1 tbsp sunflower oil
1 boneless, skinless chicken breast
2.5cm (1in) fresh ginger, grated
1 garlic clove, crushed
½ tsp ground cardamom
½ tsp ground cumin
½ tsp salt and ¼ tsp freshly ground black pepper
1 tbsp lemon juice
4 tbsp Greek-style yogurt
½ tsp paprika for sprinkling
30 coriander leaves to garnish

1 Preheat oven to 200°C (400°F/Gas 6).

2 Place the mini poppadoms in a single layer on an oiled baking sheet. Brush with oil. Bake until crisp and golden, 3–5 minutes. Cool on a wire rack.

3 Cut the chicken into thick slices (0.5cm/¼in). Combine chicken, ginger, garlic, spices, salt and pepper, lemon juice, and yogurt in a non-metallic bowl. Cover and refrigerate for at least 1 hour.

4 Preheat the grill, then grill chicken until cooked through, 8–10 minutes. Cool. Roughly chop.

5 Divide chicken evenly among the poppadoms. Sprinkle with paprika and garnish with coriander leaves. Serve chilled or at room temperature.

GET AHEAD Bake poppadoms up to 2 days in advance. Store in an airtight container at room temperature. Marinate chicken up to 1 day in advance. Cook chicken up to 1 day in advance. Cover and refrigerate. Top poppadoms up to 1 hour before serving.

COOK'S NOTE Look for mini poppadoms at speciality food halls and Indian markets. If you have difficulty finding them, this Indian-inspired topping is also delicious served on crisp tortillas.

Clams with ginger and lime butter

A seaside treat dressed up for a party, these clams are served with a ginger, lime, and coriander butter, but if you prefer, use parsley.

Makes 20

Ingredients

90g (3oz) butter, softened
1cm (½in) piece fresh ginger, finely chopped
grated zest and juice of 1 lime
1 tbsp finely chopped coriander
salt and freshly ground black pepper
20 clams
6 tbsp coarse salt

1 Combine the butter, ginger, lime, and coriander and add salt and pepper to taste.

2 Scrub the clams under running water. Discard any that are broken or not tightly closed.

3 Place the clams in a pan with 2 tbsp water and cover with a lid. Steam over medium heat until open, 6 minutes. Shake pan occasionally to ensure even cooking. Remove clams with a slotted spoon. Discard any that are shut. Cool.

4 Preheat grill. Open the clams with your fingers. Discard top shells. Loosen clams from bottom shells and place on a heatproof serving dish evenly scattered with salt. Divide the flavoured butter over the clams in their shells.

5 Place the clams under the grill until the butter melts and the clams are hot, 2 minutes. Serve hot.

GET AHEAD Make the butter up to 1 week in advance. Cover and refrigerate. Cook clams up to 1 day in advance. Cover and refrigerate. Top clams with butter up to 1 hour in advance. Grill and serve hot.

COOK'S NOTE To barbecue the clams, place unopened on a grill set 15cm (6in) above hot coals. When the shells open, the clams are done, 5 minutes. Discard top shell. Have the ginger and lime butter already melted and drizzle over the cooked clams. Cool slightly before serving or you might burn your fingers.

Gratinated mussels with parsley and Parmesan crumbs

Simple to bake and serve, these little gems can be prepared the day before. To add variety, try using another favourite hard cheese.

Makes 20

Ingredients
20 medium mussels
2 garlic cloves
2 shallots
4 tbsp olive oil
200ml (7fl oz) white wine
45g (1½oz) breadcrumbs
10g (¼oz) parsley
15g (½oz) Parmesan, grated
2 tsp grated lemon zest
salt and freshly ground black pepper

1 Clean the mussels in cold water.

2 Finely chop 1 garlic clove and 1 shallot.

3 Heat 1 tablespoon oil in a medium saucepan and sauté the chopped garlic and shallot over low heat, 2 minutes. Pour in the wine, add the mussels, cover, and cook briskly shaking the pan for 2–3 minutes until shells have opened. Tip mussels into a bowl to cool, then discard liquid or keep to use as stock.

4 Remove one of the shells from each mussel and discard, then lay the shell with mussel on a baking tray and refrigerate.

5 Place the breadcrumbs, the remaining garlic and shallot, parsley, Parmesan, and lemon zest into a food processor; pulse until well combined.

6 Preheat oven to 200°C (400°F/Gas 6).

7 Spoon the breadcrumb mixture on top of the mussels, scatter with salt and pepper, drizzle with 3 tbsp oil, and bake, 3–4 minutes. Place on a serving plate to serve.

....

GET AHEAD These can be prepared the day before, and reheated to serve.

COOK'S NOTE When cleaning the mussels, remove the beard by pulling quickly downwards.

VARIATION Use any green herb instead of parsley.

Mini Scotch eggs

Scotch eggs are well worth the effort! Best served cut in half, their layers of tasty flavours and textures are sure to impress.

Makes 10

Ingredients
10 quail's eggs
450g (1lb) sausage meat
1 tsp Dijon mustard
1 tbsp fresh thyme leaves
freshly ground black pepper
1 egg
50g (1¾oz) plain flour
40g (1½oz) fresh or panko breadcrumbs
2 litres (3½ pints) vegetable or sunflower oil

Essential equipment
deep-fat fryer or deep-sided saucepan

1 To cook the quail's eggs, place the eggs in a pan of boiling water, cover, and simmer for 1 minute. Remove from heat and allow to stand for a further minute. Drain immediately and cover with cold water.

2 Tap the eggs on a hard surface to crack shell. Pick at shell and carefully peel away, rinsing the egg gently to remove any pieces of shell. Pat eggs dry.

3 Mix the sausage meat with the mustard, thyme, and pepper.

4 Whisk the egg with 2 tbsp water in a bowl. Place the flour and breadcrumbs in separate bowls. Have a small bowl of warm water ready to keep your hands damp and clean when rolling.

5 Divide the sausage meat into 10 small balls. Flatten and mound sausage meat around eggs, squeezing together, allowing no gaps. Roll the Scotch eggs in flour, then in egg, and then in breadcrumbs. Chill until ready to fry.

6 To deep-fry, preheat the oil in a deep-fat fryer or deep-sided saucepan to 170°C (340°F/Gas 4), or until a cube of bread browns in 30 seconds. Fry in 2 batches of 5 eggs at a time for 4–5 minutes. This will allow time for the sausage meat to cook through until golden brown.

7 Serve, cut in half with mustard or herbed mayonnaise (see p88).

....

GET AHEAD Make these 24 hours before serving.

COOK'S NOTE Do not freeze. If you are not using a deep-fat fryer, you can use less oil. If you have problems finding fresh quail's eggs then buy ready-cooked hard-boiled ones.

VARIATION Use 10 dried, large pitted green or black olives instead of quail's eggs and add 1½ tsp fresh chopped rosemary and 1 tsp lemon zest to the sausage meat instead of thyme and mustard.

6 ways with **spoons**

Impress your guests with this fashionable and chic way to serve elegant bite-sized mouthfuls on stylish and contemporary spoons. Each recipe fills 20 spoons.

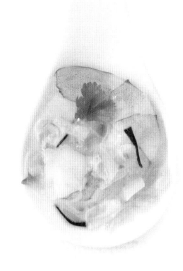

Vietnamese chicken salad

Preheat oven to 180°C (350°F/Gas 4). Poach 1 skinless chicken breast in 300ml (½ pint) milk in the oven for 20 minutes. Cool in the milk. Combine 1 seeded, chopped red chilli, 1 chopped garlic clove, 1 tbsp sugar, juice of 1 lime, 1½ tbsp fish sauce, and 1½ tbsp rice wine vinegar. Shred 50g (1¼oz) white cabbage, ¼ seeded cucumber, handful of coriander and mint, 1 seeded red chilli, 2 shallots, and 1 carrot. Slice chicken and mix with everything. Pile on each spoon and garnish with chopped peanuts.

fragrant coconut prawns

Marinate 20 raw king prawns for 1 hour in 1 finely chopped lemongrass stalk, 1 chopped shallot, 1cm (½in) piece grated ginger, 1 chopped garlic clove, pinch each of ground coriander and saffron, and 1 tbsp oil. Remove the prawns and cook the marinade for 5 minutes over low heat. Add 100ml (3½fl oz) coconut milk and salt and black pepper. Bring to a boil, add the prawns and simmer until they are cooked, about 3 minutes. Arrange 1 prawn on each spoon. Drizzle over the sauce. Garnish with coriander.

fresh crab with avocado and lemon salad

Mix 125g (4½oz) fresh white crabmeat with 1 small, ripe, diced avocado, 1 tsp finely chopped chives, 1 tsp lemon juice, 6 drops of Tabasco sauce, 4 tsp mayonnaise (see p88), 1 tsp grated lemon zest, and salt and black pepper. Taste to check the seasoning. Place 1 tsp of the salad on to each spoon and garnish with a few chervil sprigs. For a variation, replace the lemon zest and juice with lime and garnish with a few coriander leaves instead of the chervil leaves.

Know-how... how to load spoons

GET AHEAD Fill the spoons up to 30 minutes before serving.

COOK'S NOTE Do not overfill the spoons otherwise they will be difficult to handle. Choose spoons that sit well on a flat surface and are easy to pick up. Any type of spoon can be used, although ones with a curved handle and a wide head are best, such as Chinese or soup spoons. When serving spoon canapés, arrange them attractively on serving plates with the handles pointing outwards, or put them in lines on serving platters. Don't overcrowd the presentation, and provide somewhere for the empty spoons to be placed.

seared scallops, pea purée, and crisp pancetta

Preheat oven to 180°C (350°F/Gas 4). Slice off roe and white muscle from 5 large or 20 small scallops. Cut large scallops into quarters. Blanch 175g (6oz) peas for 2 minutes, drain, and purée with 2 spring onions, seasoning, 5 mint leaves, and 1 tsp crème fraîche. Crisp 5 pancetta slices in the oven. Sear the scallops in a hot frying pan with a little oil. Place ½ tsp pea purée in each spoon, add the scallops, and the pancetta to top. Garnish with lemon juice and micro amaranth or cress.

seared beef satay

Marinate 200g (7oz) beef fillet for a few hours in 1 tsp light soy sauce, 1 tsp grated ginger, and ½ tsp honey. Mix 100g (3½oz) peanut butter, 1 tbsp chilli sauce, 1 tbsp grated ginger, 3 tbsp water, and 1 tbsp light soy sauce together. Sear the steak in a hot frying pan with a dash of oil for 2 minutes on each side (or until rare) and rest for 5 minutes. Cut the steak into 20 cubes. Place a cube of beef onto each spoon, top with ½ tsp satay sauce and garnish with thin slices of red chilli and coriander.

classic prawn cocktail

Mix 250g (9oz) peeled cooked small prawns with 3 tbsp mayonnaise (see p88), 1 tsp tomato purée, ½ tbsp lemon juice, 3 drops of Tabasco sauce, 1 tsp soft brown sugar, and 1 very finely chopped spring onion. Taste to check the seasoning. Finely shred a small amount of cos lettuce, then pile some lettuce on to each spoon. Top with 1 tsp of prawn cocktail and scatter with smoked paprika to serve. For a variation, use Little Gem lettuce instead of cos and ordinary paprika instead of smoked.

Cucumber cups with blue cheese mousse and crispy bacon

This wheat-free canapé is very simple to prepare. Make the mousse up to three days ahead, but fill the cups one hour before serving.

QUICK & EASY

Makes 20

Ingredients
1 large cucumber
6 streaky bacon rashers
125g (4½oz) Roquefort cheese
125g (4½oz) cream cheese
salt and freshly ground black pepper
1 spring onion, cut into strips

Essential equipment
3.5cm (1½in) fluted cookie cutter
melon baller
piping bag with large star nozzle

1 For cucumber cups, cut cucumber into about 20 thick slices (1.5cm/¾in). Stamp each slice with the cookie cutter. Using the melon baller, scoop out soft centres to make cups, leaving a 0.5cm (¼in) layer as a base.

2 Preheat oven to 180°C (350°F/Gas 4).

3 Place bacon rashers on a foil-lined oven tray. Cook until golden and crisp, about 10–15 minutes. Drain on paper towels and cut into small triangular pieces.

4 Beat cheeses until smoothly blended. Add salt and pepper to taste.

5 Fill piping bag with mousse and pipe into cucumber cups. Top with crispy bacon pieces. Garnish with spring onion strips.

GET AHEAD Prepare mousse up to 3 days in advance. Cover and refrigerate. Cook bacon up to 1 day in advance. Store in an airtight container in the refrigerator. Crisp in a preheated 180°C (350°F/Gas 4) oven for 2 minutes. Fill cups up to 1 hour before serving.

Cucumber barquettes with smoked salmon and pickled ginger

The cucumber base can be prepared the day before, which makes these canapés very quick to assemble just before the party.

QUICK & EASY

Makes 20

Ingredients
1 cucumber
100g (3½oz) smoked salmon slices
20 pieces of pickled ginger
1 tsp wasabi

1 For cucumber barquettes, peel and cut the cucumber in half. Cut each half into 5cm (2in) length pieces. Use the tip of a knife to trim off 0.5cm (¼in) of flesh from the inside of each piece. Cut each piece into a diamond shape, about 5cm (2in) across.

2 Cut salmon into 20 wide strips (0.5cm/¼in).

3 Put a piece of ginger on top of each salmon strip and roll up.

4 Put a dab of wasabi on each cucumber boat. Top with a smoked salmon roll.

GET AHEAD Fill barquettes up to 1 hour before serving.

VARIATION Garnish with sesame seeds or julienne of red chilli.

Cherry tomatoes with crab and tarragon mayonnaise

These simple crab-stuffed cherry tomatoes are a gluten-free treat. Try not to overfill them as they may topple over when you are serving.

QUICK & EASY

Makes 20

Ingredients
20 cherry tomatoes
250g (9oz) white crab meat
4 tbsp mayonnaise (see p88)
1 tsp creamy Dijon mustard
1 tbsp chopped tarragon leaves
salt and freshly ground
black pepper

1 Cut and discard thin slices from stalk end of the tomatoes to make flat, stable bases.

2 Cut and reserve thin slices from smooth end to make tomato lids.

3 Scoop out seeds with a teaspoon and discard. Turn tomatoes upside down on paper towels to drain for 5 minutes.

4 Combine crab, mayonnaise, mustard, and tarragon. Add salt and pepper to taste.

5 Use a teaspoon to fill tomatoes with crab mixture. Top with tomato lids.

GET AHEAD Prepare tomatoes up to 2 days in advance. Store in an airtight container in the refrigerator. Fill tomatoes up to 3 hours before serving. Cover and refrigerate.

VARIATION Use a lemon mayonnaise (see p88).

Radish cups with black olive tapenade

With delicious crisp radishes and a rich salty tapenade, this healthy canapé can be made with or without anchovies.

Makes 20

Ingredients

150g (5½oz) pitted black olives
4 anchovy fillets
2 tbsp capers
1 garlic clove, finely chopped
1 tsp lemon juice
1 tsp finely chopped thyme
2 tbsp olive oil
¼ tsp freshly ground
black pepper
20 round radishes

Essential equipment
melon baller

1 Place the olives, anchovies, capers, garlic, lemon juice, thyme, and oil in a food processor or blender; pulse to a thick paste. Add pepper to season the tapenade.

2 Cut and discard thin slices from the radish bottoms to make flat, stable bases. Cut and reserve thin slices from radish tops to make radish lids.

3 Using melon baller, remove most of the radish centre to make "cups". Fill cups with tapenade. Top with reserved radish lids.

GET AHEAD Make filling up to 1 month in advance. Cover and refrigerate. Prepare cups up to 2 days in advance. Store in an airtight container in the refrigerator. Fill cups up to 1 hour before serving.

COOK'S NOTE If you don't have radishes with tops, a sprig of dill will make a decorative and flavourful alternative garnish.

Eggs Benedict

Serve this delicious canapé hot with fresh herbs, or replace the ham with wilted spinach, which works just as well.

Makes 24

Ingredients
6 slices medium white bread
125g (4½oz) butter, melted,
plus extra for greasing
24 quail's eggs
4 slices Parma ham
175ml (6fl oz) plain
hollandaise (see p89)
10g (¼oz) chives, finely
chopped to garnish

Essential equipment
24-hole mini muffin tin
5cm (2in) cookie cutter

1 Preheat oven to 150°C (300°F/Gas 2).

2 Brush the bread with melted butter and use the cookie cutter to stamp out 4 rounds per bread slice. Place the croutes on a baking tray and bake until crisp, 20–25 minutes. Cool.

3 To bake the quail's eggs, generously butter the mini muffin tin and crack eggs into each hole. Bake in the oven, 4 minutes. (The yolks should still be runny.) Using a teaspoon, carefully scoop eggs out of tins, onto a tray or plate to cool.

4 Increase oven temperature to 180°C (350°F/Gas 4). Place croutes (not touching) on a flat oven tray, tear the ham into 24 equal pieces, and place a piece folded on top of each croute. Place the baked egg on top and cover with 1 teaspoon of hollandaise. Bake, 4–5 minutes. Garnish with finely chopped chives.

....

GET AHEAD The croutes can be made several days ahead and stored in an airtight container. The hollandaise can be made 8 hours ahead, and stored at room temperature. The eggs can be baked the day before, covered, and refrigerated.

COOK'S NOTE All ovens differ slightly in temperature, so when baking the eggs try one first to work out the right time.

VARIATION Toasted French bread can be used as a base, as pictured.

Mini eggs Florentine Wilt 140g (5oz) fresh baby spinach in 1 tbsp olive oil, drain and use instead of the ham.

Mini eggs royal Replace the ham with smoked salmon.

sticks and skewers

Prosciutto-wrapped scallop brochettes with sauce béarnaise

This is an all-time favourite – sweet, tender scallops wrapped in cured, salty prosciutto, seared and served hot with sauce béarnaise.

Makes 20

Ingredients

For the sauce
3 tbsp white wine vinegar
6 peppercorns
1 shallot, finely chopped
1 sprig, plus 1 tsp finely chopped tarragon
1 sprig, plus 1 tsp finely chopped chervil

For the brochettes
20 queen scallops or
10 king scallops
7 very thin prosciutto slices
20 large basil leaves
½ tbsp oil (optional)

Essential equipment
20 wooden skewers (15cm/6in) presoaked in cold water

1 For the sauce, place the vinegar, peppercorns, shallot, and a sprig of tarragon and chervil in a small pan. Bring the ingredients to a boil over medium heat and continue cooking until the liquid is reduced to 1 tbsp. Cool and strain.

2 Now follow the recipe for hollandaise (see p89). Place the reduction in a bowl with the water, egg yolks, and salt and pepper and follow the recipe method.

3 Stir in 1 tsp each of finely chopped tarragon and chervil after the butter has been added. Adjust seasoning, adding more salt and pepper to taste.

4 For the brochettes, if using king scallops, slice in half crossways. Cut each prosciutto slice into 3 strips.

5 Place 1 basil leaf on top of each prosciutto strip. Place 1 queen scallop or ½ king scallop on top. Wrap basil and prosciutto around each scallop. Secure each wrapped scallop with 1 presoaked skewer.

6 Preheat grill. Alternatively, preheat a heavy frying pan with oil. Either grill or sear scallop brochettes until scallops have turned from opaque to white, 1–2 minutes on each side. Serve hot, warm, or at room temperature with sauce béarnaise.

....

GET AHEAD Skewer scallops up to 8 hours in advance. Store in an airtight container in the refrigerator. Skewers can be grilled or seared 1 hour in advance, placed on an oven tray, covered with foil, and reheated in a hot oven for 5 minutes to serve.

VARIATION Replace prosciutto with thinly sliced pancetta.

Grapefruit scallop ceviche skewers

The scallops need at least three hours to marinate, which gives you plenty of time to get ahead.

Makes 20

Ingredients
40 queen scallops or
20 king scallops
grated zest and
juice of 1 grapefruit
juice of 2 limes
4 tbsp olive oil
1 fresh red chilli, seeded
and finely chopped
½ red onion, finely chopped
½ tsp salt
1 tbsp finely chopped coriander
1 spring onion, finely sliced

Essential equipment
20 wooden skewers or
toothpicks (7.5cm/3in)

1 If using king scallops, slice in half crossways.

2 Combine scallops, grapefruit, lime, oil, chilli, onion, and salt in a non-metallic bowl. Cover and refrigerate for 3 hours, stirring occasionally.

3 Remove scallops with a slotted spoon. Toss to coat with coriander and spring onion. Thread 2 queen scallops or 2 king scallop halves on to each skewer. Serve chilled with herbed yogurt dip (see p91).

GET AHEAD Marinate scallops up to 6 hours in advance. Skewer scallops up to 3 hours in advance. Store in an airtight container in the refrigerator.

COOK'S NOTE If you are uncomfortable about serving raw fish, use cooked, peeled tiger prawns instead of raw scallops.

Tangy Thai prawn skewers

These fabulous tiger prawns are marinated in a fusion of Thai flavours that can be prepared up to three hours before serving.

Makes 20

Ingredients

20 tiger prawns, cooked
and peeled
2 garlic cloves, finely chopped
1cm (½in) piece fresh
ginger, grated
1 red chilli, seeded and
finely chopped
1 tsp granulated sugar
1 tbsp fish sauce
juice of 1 lime

Essential equipment

20 wooden skewers or
toothpicks (7.5cm/3in)

1 Pat the prawns dry with kitchen paper. Combine prawns, garlic, ginger, chilli, sugar, sauce, and lime juice in a non-metallic bowl. Cover and refrigerate for 1 hour.

2 Skewer 1 prawn on to each skewer. Serve chilled.

....

GET AHEAD Make marinade the day before. Marinate prawns up to 6 hours in advance. Skewer prawns up to 3 hours in advance. Store in an airtight container in the refrigerator.

Barbecued tandoori prawn sticks

A classic fragrantly spiced tandoori marinade that works just as well with chicken. Marinate the prawns for one hour before searing.

Makes 20

Ingredients

125ml (4fl oz) Greek-style yogurt
2 tbsp lemon juice
3 garlic cloves, crushed
2.5cm (1in) piece fresh ginger, grated
1 tsp turmeric
1 tsp paprika
¼ tsp ground cardamom
¼ tsp cayenne pepper
1 tsp salt
20 raw tiger prawns, peeled and deveined
½ tbsp oil (optional)

Essential equipment

20 wooden skewers or toothpicks (7.5cm/3in) presoaked in cold water

1 For the marinade, combine the yogurt, lemon juice, garlic, ginger, spices, and salt in a non-metallic bowl. Add the prawns and toss in marinade to coat each one well. Cover and refrigerate for 1 hour.

2 Thread 1 prawn on to each presoaked skewer.

3 Preheat grill. Alternatively, preheat a heavy frying pan with oil. Either grill or sear prawns until they turn pink and lose their transparency, 3 minutes on each side. Serve hot, warm, or at room temperature.

....

GET AHEAD Marinate prawns up to 4 hours in advance. Store in an airtight container in the refrigerator. Skewer prawns up to 1 hour in advance. Store in an airtight container in the refrigerator. Skewers can be grilled or seared 1 hour in advance, placed on an oven tray, covered with foil, and reheated in a hot oven for 5 minutes to serve.

COOK'S NOTE Don't forget to presoak wooden skewers when using them in a grilled recipe. Allow the skewers to soak for up to 1 hour in cold water to prevent them from scorching.

VARIATION Replace the prawns with chicken.

Monkfish, pancetta, and rosemary spiedini with lemon aïoli

Skewering the pieces of pancetta-wrapped fish on rosemary sticks will infuse the recipe with woody sweetness.

Makes 20

Ingredients
350g (12oz) monkfish tail, boned and skinned
10 long slices thin pancetta
20 rosemary branches (10cm/4in)
1 tbsp olive oil

For the marinade
4 tbsp olive oil
grated zest and juice of ½ lemon
1 garlic clove, finely chopped
½ tsp salt and ½ tsp freshly ground black pepper

1 Cut the monkfish into 20 cubes (2.5cm/1in) and cut each slice of pancetta in half lengthways.

2 To make the rosemary spiedini, strip off the leaves from the rosemary branches, leaving just a few at the top. Reserve leaves. Sharpen the other end into a point with a sharp knife.

3 For the marinade, roughly chop 1 tbsp of reserved rosemary leaves. Combine the rosemary, oil, lemon, garlic, and salt and pepper in a bowl. Add the monkfish and toss to coat fish well. Cover and refrigerate for 30 minutes.

4 Wrap each piece of monkfish tightly with a strip of pancetta and thread 1 piece on to the pointed end of a rosemary skewer.

5 Heat a heavy saucepan with 1 tbsp oil and sear the spiedini for 1 minute on each side. Serve warm with lemon aïoli (see p88).

VARIATION You can use 1 piece of prosciutto cut into 4 strips instead of the pancetta.

Salmon teriyaki skewers with ginger soy dipping sauce

The teriyaki marinade works especially well with salmon fillet. Once grilled and cooked, serve with this sharp gingery dipping sauce.

Makes 20

Ingredients
350g (12oz) salmon fillet,
2.5cm (1in) thick
½ tbsp oil (optional)

For the glaze
3 tbsp sake
3 tbsp mirin
5 tbsp shoyu
(Japanese soy sauce)
1½ tbsp caster sugar

For the sauce
1cm (½in) piece fresh ginger,
finely chopped
2 spring onions, finely sliced
juice of 2 limes
6 tbsp shoyu
(Japanese soy sauce)

Essential equipment
20 wooden skewers or
chopsticks (15cm/6in)
presoaked in cold water

1 Cut the salmon into 20 cubes (2.5cm/1in).

2 For glaze, place the sake, mirin, soy, and sugar in a small pan. Bring to a boil over medium heat. Simmer gently for 10 minutes until thick and syrupy. Cool.

3 For the sauce, whisk the ginger, spring onions, lime, and soy together. Let stand at room temperature for 15 minutes to allow the flavours to blend.

4 Toss salmon with cooled glaze in a non-metallic bowl to coat each piece well. Leave to marinate at room temperature for 10 minutes. Thread 1 salmon cube on to each skewer or chopstick.

5 Preheat grill. Alternatively, preheat a heavy frying pan with oil. Either grill or sear the salmon skewers until firm to the touch, 2–3 minutes on each side. Serve hot or warm with ginger soy dipping sauce.

....

GET AHEAD Skewer salmon up to 3 hours in advance. Store in an airtight container in the refrigerator. Make dipping sauce without spring onions up to 3 days in advance. Cover and refrigerate. Add spring onions up to 3 hours before serving. Keep covered at room temperature. Skewers can be grilled or seared 1 hour in advance, placed on an oven tray, covered with foil, and reheated in a hot oven for 5 minutes to serve.

Chargrilled Mediterranean tuna skewers with spicy roast tomato dip

With fresh tuna, basil leaves, lemon, and plum tomatoes, this wonderful canapé bursts with the flavours of the Mediterranean.

Makes 20

Ingredients
350g (12oz) tuna steak, 2.5cm (1in) thick
½ tbsp oil (optional)

For the marinade
15g (½oz) basil
15g (½oz) parsley
2 garlic cloves
grated zest and juice of ½ lemon
2 tbsp olive oil
1 tsp salt and ½ tsp freshly ground black pepper
20 large basil leaves

For the dip
6 plum tomatoes, halved
1 red chilli, seeded and chopped
2 garlic cloves, chopped
1 tbsp olive oil
1 tbsp balsamic vinegar
salt and freshly ground black pepper

Essential equipment
20 wooden skewers (15cm/6in) presoaked in cold water

1 Cut tuna into 2.5cm (1in) cubes.

2 For the marinade, place the basil, parsley, garlic, lemon, oil, and salt and pepper in a food processor or blender; pulse to a thick paste.

3 Toss tuna and marinade together in a non-metallic bowl to coat each piece well. Cover and refrigerate for at least 30 minutes.

4 For the dip, preheat oven to 200°C (400°F/Gas 6). Place the tomatoes on an oven tray. Sprinkle over chilli, garlic, oil, vinegar, and a pinch of salt and pepper. Roast until softened, 30 minutes.

5 Place in a food processor or blender; pulse until smooth. Push through a sieve to remove seeds. Add salt and pepper to taste. Keep warm.

6 Wrap each tuna cube in a basil leaf. Thread 1 wrapped tuna cube on to each presoaked skewer.

7 Preheat grill. Alternatively, preheat a heavy frying pan with oil. Either grill or sear tuna skewers until cooked through, 2–3 minutes on each side. Serve hot or warm with spicy roast tomato dip.

....

GET AHEAD Make dip up to 2 days in advance. Cover and refrigerate. Marinate tuna up to 4 hours in advance. Store in an airtight container in the refrigerator. Skewer up to 2 hours in advance. Store in an airtight container in the refrigerator. Reheat dip just before serving. Skewers can be grilled or seared 1 hour in advance, placed on an oven tray, covered with foil, and reheated in a hot oven for 5 minutes to serve.

COOK'S NOTE Oven roasting tomatoes concentrates their flavour and is a very good treatment for out of season or less than ripe tomatoes.

Moroccan-spiced swordfish brochettes

This firm-fleshed fish is popular in the Mediterranean. It can withstand this robust Moroccan marinade, making it an unusual party canapé.

Makes 20

Ingredients
350g (12oz) swordfish steak, 2.5cm (1in) thick

For the marinade
1 red pepper, quartered and seeded
1 red chilli, seeded and chopped
2 garlic cloves, chopped
2 tbsp chopped coriander
2 tbsp chopped parsley
½ tsp ground coriander
1 tsp runny honey
grated zest and juice of ½ lemon
2 tbsp olive oil
1 tsp salt and ¼ tsp freshly ground black pepper
½ tbsp oil (optional)

Essential equipment
20 wooden skewers (15cm/6in) presoaked in cold water

1 Cut the swordfish into 20 cubes (2.5cm/1in).

2 For the marinade, grill and peel the pepper quarters (see p92, Steps 1 and 2). Place peeled pepper quarters, chilli, garlic, fresh herbs, ground coriander, honey, lemon, oil, and salt and pepper in a food processor or blender; pulse to a thick paste.

3 Toss swordfish and marinade together in a non-metallic bowl to coat each piece well. Cover and refrigerate for at least 30 minutes.

4 Thread 1 swordfish cube on to each presoaked skewer.

5 Preheat grill. Alternatively, preheat a heavy frying pan with oil. Either grill or fry swordfish brochettes until cooked through, 2–3 minutes on each side. Serve hot or warm.

....

GET AHEAD Marinate swordfish up to 4 hours in advance. Store in an airtight container in the refrigerator. Skewer up to 2 hours in advance. Store in an airtight container in the refrigerator. Skewers can be grilled or seared 1 hour in advance, placed on an oven tray, covered with foil, and reheated in a hot oven for 5 minutes to serve.

VARIATION If swordfish is not available, monkfish, king prawns, or other firm-fleshed fish can be used.

Curried coconut chicken sticks

These chicken skewers are packed so full with succulent flavours that they will become an all-time party favourite.

Makes 20

Ingredients
2 boneless, skinless chicken breasts

For the marinade
4 lemongrass stalks
1 tbsp curry powder
4 garlic cloves, chopped
5cm (2in) piece fresh ginger, chopped
1 tbsp soft brown sugar
2 shallots, chopped
15g (½oz) coriander
4 tbsp fish sauce
125ml (4fl oz) tinned coconut milk
1 tsp salt and ¼ tsp freshly ground black pepper
½ tbsp oil (optional)

Essential equipment
20 wooden skewers (15cm/6in) presoaked in cold water

1 Cut the chicken into 20 cubes (2.5cm/1in).

2 For the marinade, remove and discard the tough outer skin from the lemongrass stalks and finely chop. Place lemongrass, curry powder, garlic, ginger, sugar, shallots, coriander, fish sauce, coconut milk, and salt and pepper in a food processor or blender; pulse until smooth.

3 Toss chicken and marinade together in a non-metallic bowl to coat each piece well. Cover and refrigerate for at least 1 hour.

4 Thread 1 chicken cube on to each presoaked skewer. Preheat grill. Alternatively, preheat a heavy frying pan with oil. Either grill or fry chicken sticks until cooked through, 5 minutes on each side. Serve hot, warm, or at room temperature.

....

GET AHEAD Marinate chicken up to 1 day in advance. Skewer chicken up to 12 hours in advance. Store in an airtight container in the refrigerator. Skewers can be grilled or seared 1 hour in advance, placed on an oven tray, covered with foil, and reheated in a hot oven for 5 minutes to serve.

6 ways with **skewers**

This is an ideal way to serve marinated fish, meats, and wrapped food. Threading bite-sized pieces onto skewers makes them easy to prepare and eat. These recipes make 20.

stuffed medjool dates wrapped in prosciutto

Cut 10 medjool dates in half and remove and discard the stones. Spread 30g (1oz) Gorgonzola or other blue cheese over the cut side of each date. Cut 5 slices of prosciutto or Parma ham into 4 long slices. Roll up the dates inside a strip of the prosciutto with ½ basil leaf. Thread onto wooden skewers and serve at room temperature. Alternatively, quickly flash fry in a little olive oil and serve the skewers warm.

marinated king prawns wrapped in mangetout

Marinate 20 peeled king prawns in 1 tsp grated lemon zest, a little salt and pepper, 1 tsp olive oil, 1 tsp lemon juice, and a pinch of cayenne pepper. Blanch 20 large mangetout in boiling salted water for 1 minute, drain, refresh in cold water, and pat dry. Thread 1 end of the mangetout onto a skewer, then a prawn followed by the other end of the mangetout. Serve with aïoli or another flavoured mayonnaise (see p88).

lamb fillet with pomegranate and mint

Cut 300g (10oz) lamb loin into 20 (2.5cm/1in) cubes. Combine 2 tbsp finely chopped mint, 1 chopped garlic clove, 2 tsp olive oil, and 2 tsp pomegranate molasses. Pour over the lamb and chill for at least 1 hour, preferably overnight. Heat a frying pan with 1 tbsp olive oil and sear the lamb in batches over high heat for 1 minute on each side. Rest for 2 minutes then serve on a wooden skewer.

Know-how... choosing and using skewers

COOK'S NOTE If using wooden skewers soak them in cold water for at least 1 hour before use to avoid burning when cooking. Always load the skewered food at the end of each skewer so your guests can eat the mouthful easily. If you are just using the skewers for serving there are plenty of stylish, decorative bamboo or wooden skewers to choose from unusual designs, such as ones with elegant loops, twists, heart, or paddle shapes at the ends.

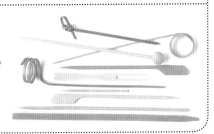

marinated bocconcini with cherry tomatoes and basil

Dry 20 bocconcini mozzarella (baby mozzarella balls) and marinate in a pinch of paprika, a grinding of black pepper, 1 tsp grated lemon zest, and 1 tsp olive oil. Cut 10 cherry vine tomatoes in half widthways. For each skewer, thread on the tomato, then one end of a basil leaf, then the bocconcini, and finally the other end of the basil leaf. Cover well with cling film and leave in a cool place until ready to serve.

Thai chicken

Slice 2 boneless, skinless chicken breasts into 20 slices. Combine 3 tbsp sweet chilli dipping sauce, 1 tbsp lime juice, 2 tsp grated lime zest, and a handful of chopped coriander. Pour the marinade over the chicken and chill for at least 2 hours, preferably overnight. Thread 1 piece of chicken onto presoaked wooden skewers. Sear the chicken on the skewers in 1 tbsp sunflower oil for 5 minutes on each side until cooked. Serve with chilli dipping sauce, coriander leaves, and lime wedges.

bresaola wrapped figs with rocket and Parmesan

Cut 5 slices of thin bresaola into 4 strips lengthways. Roll up 20 mini pickled figs inside the bresaola using a handful of rocket leaves and Parmesan shavings. Thread onto the end of a wooden skewer and serve chilled or at room temperature. If you can't find mini pickled figs you can use large pickled figs, cut in half or quarters. Replace the bresaola with Parma ham, if you prefer.

Thai chicken and lemongrass sticks with sweet cucumber dipping sauce

Fresh lemongrass sticks are used as skewers for these mini Thai-inspired chicken patties. Make sure the chicken is cooked through before serving.

Makes 20

Ingredients

11 lemongrass stalks
2 boneless, skinless chicken breasts
2 garlic cloves, chopped
1 red chilli, seeded and chopped
2 tbsp chopped coriander
1 tsp brown sugar
1 tsp salt
½ tbsp oil (optional)

For the sauce

125ml (4fl oz) rice vinegar
125g (4½oz) granulated sugar
2 garlic cloves, finely chopped
2 red chillies, seeded and finely chopped
½ tsp salt
¼ cucumber, seeded and finely diced
1 tbsp finely chopped coriander

1 For the lemongrass sticks, remove and discard the tough outer skin from the lemongrass.

2 Finely chop 1 stalk then set aside to flavour the chicken. Cut each of the 10 remaining lemongrass stalks in half lengthways, keeping the stalks attached by the root. Trim to 12.5cm (5in) lengths.

3 Place the reserved chopped lemongrass stalk, chicken, garlic, chilli, coriander, sugar, and salt in a food processor; pulse to a smooth paste. Divide into 20 equal-sized pieces. With wet hands, roll into oval shapes. Skewer each chicken oval on to the thicker end of each lemongrass length. Cover and refrigerate for 30 minutes to allow the flavours to blend.

4 For the sauce, bring the vinegar and sugar to a boil in a pan over medium heat. Simmer gently until syrupy, 5 minutes. Pour syrup over the garlic, chillies, and salt in a separate bowl and cool.

5 When cool, stir in the cucumber and coriander. Let stand for 15 minutes at room temperature to allow the flavours to combine.

6 Preheat grill. Alternatively, preheat a heavy frying pan with oil. Either grill or sear chicken lemongrass sticks until cooked through, 5 minutes on each side. Serve hot, warm, or at room temperature with sweet cucumber dipping sauce.

GET AHEAD Lemongrass sticks can be prepared 2 days in advance. Prepare and skewer chicken up to 12 hours in advance. Store in an airtight container in the refrigerator. Make sauce without cucumber and coriander up to 3 days in advance. Cover and refrigerate. Add cucumber and coriander up to 3 hours before serving. Keep covered at room temperature. Skewers can be grilled or seared 1 hour in advance, placed on an oven tray, covered with foil, and reheated in a hot oven for 5 minutes to serve.

Chicken yakitori

Use chicken thighs, which are full of flavour, as the base for this Japanese sweet soy marinade. Serve with shiitake mushrooms and spring onions.

Makes 20

Ingredients
350g (12oz) boneless, skinless chicken thighs
½ tbsp oil (optional)

For the marinade
4 tbsp shoyu (Japanese soy sauce)
2 tbsp mirin
1½ tbsp sake
1 tsp caster sugar
5 shiitake mushrooms
2 spring onions

Essential equipment
20 wooden skewers (15cm/6in) presoaked in cold water

1 Cut the chicken into 20 pieces (2.5cm/1in).

2 For the marinade, place the soy, mirin, sake, and sugar in a small pan. Bring to a boil over medium heat. Simmer gently until slightly syrupy, 5 minutes. Cool.

3 Toss the marinade and chicken together in a non-metallic bowl to coat each piece well. Cover and refrigerate for at least 30 minutes.

4 Cut the mushrooms into quarters. Cut the spring onions in 20 lengths (2.5cm/1in).

5 Thread 1 spring onion piece, 1 chicken cube, and 1 mushroom quarter on to each presoaked skewer. Preheat grill. Alternatively, preheat a heavy frying pan with oil. Either grill or sear chicken yakitori until cooked through, 5 minutes on each side. Serve hot.

....

GET AHEAD Marinate chicken up to 3 hours in advance. Assemble skewers up to 1 hour in advance. Store in an airtight container in the refrigerator. Skewers can be grilled or seared 1 hour in advance, placed on an oven tray, covered with foil, and reheated in a hot oven for 5 minutes to serve.

Fennel-marinated feta and olive skewers

As this recipe tastes so fresh and clean, it will work well with richer dishes. It makes a delicious vegetarian option.

Makes 20

Ingredients
2 tbsp sesame seeds
200g (7oz) feta cheese
1 tbsp fennel seeds
grated zest of 1 lemon
1 tbsp lemon juice
2 tbsp olive oil
1½ tsp cracked black pepper
15g (½oz) mint, finely chopped
½ cucumber, peeled and seeded
20 mint leaves
10 pitted black olives, halved

Essential equipment
20 wooden skewers (5cm/2in)

1 Toast the seeds in a dry pan over low heat until nutty and golden, 3 minutes. Cool.

2 Gently rinse the feta in cold water. Drain on paper towels.

3 Cut feta into 2cm (¾in) cubes. Toss feta together with the fennel, toasted seeds, lemon zest and juice, oil, and pepper to coat each cube well. Cover and refrigerate for 4 hours to allow the flavours to combine.

4 Sprinkle the feta with chopped mint and toss to coat each cube well.

5 Cut the cucumber into 20 cubes (1cm/½in).

6 Thread 1 mint leaf, 1 olive half, 1 cucumber cube, and 1 feta cube onto each skewer. Serve chilled or at room temperature.

....

GET AHEAD Marinate the feta up to 3 days in advance. Store in an airtight container in the refrigerator. Skewer feta up to 4 hours in advance. Cover and refrigerate.

Lime-marinated chicken skewers with avocado crème dip

These tender cubes of chicken are marinated in sweet honey, lime, chillies, and coriander. Serve with a smooth, rich dip of avocado and sour cream.

Makes 20

Ingredients
2 boneless, skinless chicken breasts
½ tbsp oil (optional)

For the marinade
juice of 1 lime
1 tbsp runny honey
2 tbsp olive oil
2 green chillies, seeded and finely chopped
15g (½oz) coriander, finely chopped
1 tsp salt and ¼ tsp freshly ground black pepper

For the dip
1 avocado, stoned
3 spring onions, chopped
1 tbsp red wine vinegar
1 tbsp olive oil
125ml (4fl oz) sour cream
salt and freshly ground black pepper

To garnish
1 tbsp finely chopped coriander

Essential equipment
20 wooden skewers (15cm/6in) presoaked in cold water

1 Cut the chicken into cubes (2.5cm/1in).

2 For marinade, combine lime, honey, oil, chillies, coriander, and salt and pepper in a non-metallic bowl. Add chicken and toss to coat each piece well. Cover and refrigerate for at least 1 hour.

3 For dip, place avocado, spring onions, vinegar, oil, and sour cream in a food processor or blender; pulse until smooth. Add salt and pepper to taste. Cover and refrigerate for 30 minutes to allow the flavours to blend.

4 Thread a chicken cube on to each presoaked skewer. Preheat grill. Alternatively, preheat a heavy frying pan with oil. Either grill or sear chicken skewers until cooked through, 5 minutes on each side. Garnish each skewer with a sprinkling of coriander. Serve warm with avocado crème dip.

....

GET AHEAD Marinate chicken up to 1 day in advance. Skewer chicken up to 12 hours in advance. Store in an airtight container in the refrigerator. Make dip up to 8 hours in advance. Cover and refrigerate. Skewers can be grilled or seared 1 hour in advance, placed on an oven tray, covered with foil, and reheated in a hot oven for 5 minutes to serve.

COOK'S NOTE To prevent the avocado crème dip from discolouring when making ahead, make sure you press a piece of cling film directly on to the surface of the dip. It's the oxygen in the air that turns avocado brown, so the less air that comes into contact with the dip, the better.

Spicy satay sticks

You can leave the chicken to marinate overnight, and the sauce can also be made days ahead. It is so good I suggest doubling the recipe.

Makes 20

Ingredients
2 boneless, skinless chicken breasts
½ tbsp oil (optional)

For the marinade
1 lemongrass stalk
2 shallots
2 garlic cloves
1cm (½in) piece fresh ginger
2 tsp brown sugar
½ tsp ground cumin
1 tsp turmeric
½ tsp ground coriander
1 tsp salt
1 tbsp sunflower oil

For the sauce
4 tbsp roasted peanuts
2 lemongrass stalks
2 shallots
2 garlic cloves
2.5cm (1in) piece fresh ginger
1 tsp turmeric
1 tbsp sunflower oil
1 tbsp brown sugar
1 tsp fish sauce
1 tbsp Chinese hot chilli sauce
juice of 1 lime
4 tbsp water
125ml (4fl oz) coconut milk

Essential equipment
20 wooden skewers (15cm/6in) presoaked in cold water

1 Slice the chicken into 20 strips (0.5cm/¼in thick and 6cm/2½in long).

2 For the marinade, remove and discard the tough outer skin from the lemongrass and finely chop. Place lemongrass, shallots, garlic, ginger, sugar, spices, turmeric, salt, and oil in a food processor or blender; pulse to a smooth paste. Toss chicken and marinade together in a non-metallic bowl to coat each piece well. Cover and refrigerate for at least 1 hour.

3 For the sauce, place the peanuts in a food processor or blender; pulse until finely ground. Set aside.

4 Remove and discard the tough outer skin from the lemongrass and finely chop. Place the shallots, garlic, ginger, chopped lemongrass, turmeric, and oil in a food processor or blender; pulse to a smooth paste.

5 Heat a frying pan over medium heat. Add paste and stir fry until softened, 5 minutes. Stir in ground peanuts, sugar, fish sauce, chilli sauce, lime, water, and coconut milk. Cook, stirring occasionally, until the sauce thickens, 10 minutes. Keep warm.

6 Thread 1 chicken strip on to each presoaked skewer, running the skewer through it like a ruffled ribbon.

7 Preheat grill. Alternatively, preheat a heavy frying pan with oil. Either grill or sear chicken satay sticks until cooked through, 5 minutes on each side. Serve hot with warm satay sauce.

....

GET AHEAD Make sauce up to 4 days in advance. Cover and refrigerate. Marinate chicken up to 1 day in advance. Skewer chicken up to 12 hours in advance. Store in an airtight container in the refrigerator. Reheat sauce before serving. Skewers can be kept warm in low oven until ready to serve.

COOK'S NOTE The satay sauce will thicken on standing so if making ahead, bear in mind that you may need to thin it down with a tablespoon or so of lime juice or water when you reheat.

Cumin-scented kofte brochettes with minted yogurt dip

Add your own favourite spices to the minced lamb and shape into koftes. These are perfect for a summer party served with the minted yogurt dip.

Makes 20

Ingredients

For the brochettes
350g (12oz) lean minced lamb
1 medium onion, grated
2 garlic cloves, chopped
2 tsp ground cumin
½ tsp ground coriander
grated zest of 1 lemon
2 tbsp finely chopped coriander
1½ tsp salt
¼ tsp cayenne pepper
½ tbsp oil (optional)

For the dip
175ml (6fl oz) Greek-style yogurt
15g (½oz) mint, finely chopped
15g (½oz) parsley, finely chopped
juice of ½ lemon
salt
cayenne pepper

Essential equipment
20 wooden skewers (15cm/6in) presoaked in cold water

1 For the brochettes, place the lamb, onion, garlic, cumin, ground coriander, lemon, fresh coriander, and salt and pepper in a food processor; pulse until combined and slighly pasty. Divide into 20 equal-sized pieces. With wet hands, roll into oval shapes. Thread 1 oval on to each presoaked skewer. Cover and refrigerate for 30 minutes.

2 For the dip, combine the yogurt, mint, parsley, and lemon juice. Add salt and pepper to taste. Cover and refrigerate for 30 minutes to allow the flavours to blend.

3 Preheat grill. Alternatively, preheat a heavy frying pan with oil. Either grill or sear brochettes until browned but still pink and juicy inside, 3 minutes on each side. Serve hot with chilled minted yogurt dip.

....

GET AHEAD Make dip up to 1 day in advance. Cover and refrigerate. Prepare and skewer kofte up to 12 hours in advance. Store in an airtight container in the refrigerator. Skewers can be grilled or seared 1 hour in advance, placed on an oven tray, covered with foil, and reheated in a hot oven for 5 minutes to serve.

Sesame soy glazed beef skewers

This is a real treat, using tender beef fillet marinated in hot chilli sauce, sesame, lemongrass, and honey. Sear briefly to serve rare.

Makes 20

Ingredients
350g (12oz) beef fillet or sirloin,
2.5cm (1in) thick
4 spring onions, white stalk only
1 red pepper, halved and seeded
½ tbsp oil (optional)

For the glaze
2 lemongrass stalks, tender
stalk only, finely chopped
1 tbsp runny honey
2 tbsp sesame oil
1 tbsp sunflower oil
2 tbsp light soy sauce
1 tbsp Chinese hot chilli sauce
1 tsp salt and ½ tsp freshly
ground black pepper

To garnish
2 tbsp sesame seeds

Essential equipment
20 wooden skewers (15cm/6in)
presoaked in cold water

1 Cut the beef into 20 cubes (2.5cm/1in). Cut the spring onions diagonally into 20 lengths (2.5cm/1in). Cut the pepper into 20 pieces (2.5cm/1in).

2 For the glaze, combine the lemongrass, honey, oils, soy, chilli sauce, and salt and pepper in a non-metallic bowl. Add beef, spring onions, and pepper. Toss to coat each piece well. Cover and refrigerate for at least 1 hour.

3 Thread 1 piece each of spring onion and pepper and 1 beef cube on to each presoaked skewer.

4 Preheat grill. Alternatively, preheat a heavy frying pan with oil. Either grill or sear beef skewers until browned but still pink and juicy inside, 3 minutes on each side. Sprinkle with sesame seeds and serve hot.

GET AHEAD Marinate beef up to 1 day in advance. Store in an airtight container in the refrigerator. Skewer beef up to 12 hours in advance. Store in an airtight container in the refrigerator. Skewers can be grilled or seared 1 hour in advance, placed on an oven tray, covered with foil, and reheated in a hot oven for 5 minutes to serve.

Asian pork balls with chilli-lime dipping sauce

Meatballs are a great party food – they are versatile, packed with flavour, and delicious served with various dipping sauces.

Makes 20

Ingredients

For the sauce
juice of 1 lime
1 tbsp caster sugar
2 tbsp fish sauce
1 red chilli, seeded and finely chopped
1 garlic clove, finely chopped
1 tbsp grated fresh root ginger

For the meatballs
200g (7oz) minced pork
30g (1oz) shallots, finely diced
2 garlic cloves, finely diced
1 tsp soft brown sugar
½ tsp freshly ground black pepper
10g (¼oz) coriander leaves, finely chopped
10g (¼oz) mint leaves, finely chopped
1 tbsp grated fresh ginger
2 tbsp Thai fish sauce
vegetable or sunflower oil to fry

To garnish
1 tbsp chopped fresh coriander

Essential equipment
large non-stick frying pan

1 For the sauce, mix all the ingredients together with 2 tbsp water and taste for seasoning.

2 Place the meatball ingredients into a large bowl. Mix well together and mould 1 ball into the size of a walnut for testing.

3 Heat a frying pan with 2 tbsp of oil and fry the ball on both sides for 2 minutes or until cooked through. Taste to check flavour. You may wish to add more fish sauce or salt. Roll the remainder of the mixture into small balls.

4 Fry briskly but gently on both sides to cook through. At this stage you can keep them warm in a medium oven until ready to serve. Serve with the chilli-lime dipping sauce scattered with torn coriander.

....

GET AHEAD The pork balls can be made several days ahead or frozen for 1 month.

VARIATION

Eastern lamb balls with pistachio and harissa Replace the pork with 200g (7oz) minced lamb and add ½ onion, finely chopped; zest of 1 lemon; 1 garlic clove, finely chopped; 1½ tsp harissa paste; 10g (¼oz) parsley, finely chopped; 30g (1oz) pistachios, finely chopped; 1 egg; salt and freshly ground black pepper. Mix well and proceed as in the main recipe. Serve with roast pepper, feta, and mint dip (see p93).

Mediterranean meatballs with lemon, Parmesan, and gremolata Replace the pork with 200g (7oz) beef mince and add 1 garlic clove, finely chopped; 1 tbsp chopped rosemary; zest of 1 lemon; 1 egg; salt and pepper to taste; 75g (2½oz) Parmesan, grated; 1 shallot, finely chopped. Mix well together and proceed as in the main recipe. Serve with gremolata sprinkled over. To make gremolata, mix together 1 tbsp chopped parsley; 1 tbsp lemon zest; and 1 garlic clove, grated.

dips, dippers, and soup shots

Mayonnaise

An essential party ingredient, mayonnaise is used in many of the canapés. Use ready-made mayonnaise when short of time.

Makes 300ml (10fl oz)

Ingredients
2 egg yolks
1 tsp creamy Dijon mustard
1 tbsp white wine vinegar
½ tsp salt and a pinch of freshly ground black pepper
1 tsp sugar
300ml (10fl oz) sunflower oil

Essential equipment
wire whisk

Safety warning on raw eggs
Because of the potential risk of salmonella, pregnant women, young children, and anyone with a weakened immune system should avoid eating raw eggs. Make sure you use only the freshest (preferably organic) eggs, and, if in doubt, substitute ready-made mayonnaise.

1 Set a deep bowl on a cloth to prevent it from slipping as you whisk. Whisk the egg yolks, mustard, vinegar, salt and pepper, and sugar together until thick and creamy, 1 minute.

2 Place the oil in a jug. Whisk in the oil a drop at a time until the mixture thickens.

3 Add the remaining oil in a thin, steady stream, whisking constantly until thick and glossy. Whisk in any flavouring, if using. Adjust seasoning to taste.

GET AHEAD Make mayonnaise 3 days ahead and store covered in the refrigerator. Return to room temperature and stir to serve.

COOK'S NOTE If the mayonnaise separates, combine 1 tsp white wine vinegar and 1 tsp Dijon mustard and whisk in the separated mayonnaise drop by drop until the mixture re-emulsifies.

VARIATION
Lemon mayonnaise Whisk 1 tbsp each lemon juice and zest into mayonnaise.

Aïoli/Lemon aïoli Whisk 2 crushed garlic cloves into mayonnaise/ lemon mayonnaise.

Tartar Whisk 1 tbsp each finely chopped tarragon, parsley, and capers into mayonnaise.

Mustard mayonnaise Add 1 tbsp English mustard or wholegrain mustard and 1 tbsp cold water to mayonnaise.

Chilli-lime mayonnaise Whisk 1 tbsp lime juice, 1 tbsp lime zest, and 1 red chilli, seeded and finely chopped into mayonnaise.

Herb mayonnaise Add 1 tbsp each of finely chopped basil, watercress, and tarragon to mayonnaise.

Lemon hollandaise

Lemon juice balances the rich flavour of this French classic. Make sure that the eggs are not over a high heat, otherwise they will scramble.

Makes 175ml (6fl oz)

Ingredients
125g (4½oz) butter
2 tbsp water
2 egg yolks
salt and
white pepper
juice of ½ lemon

1 Melt the butter, then skim the froth from the surface with a spoon. Leave to cool until tepid.

2 Place a heatproof bowl over a pan of simmering water set on low heat. Make sure the base of the bowl is not in direct contact with the hot water. Place water and yolks with a pinch of salt and pepper in the bowl.

3 Whisk the ingredients to a light and frothy mixture that holds the trail of the whisk, 3 minutes. Remove the pan from the heat.

4 Whisk in butter, a little at a time, whisking vigorously after each addition, until the mixture emulsifies and becomes thick and creamy. Gradually whisk in the lemon juice. Adjust seasoning, adding more salt and pepper, or lemon juice to taste.

....

GET AHEAD Make hollandaise up to 30 minutes in advance. Keep warm in a bowl over a pan of hot water placed off the heat. Alternatively, make hollandaise up to 2 days in advance. Cover and refrigerate. Place in a heatproof bowl over a pan of simmering water set over low heat. Make sure the base of the bowl is not in direct contact with the water. Warm through, whisking occasionally, until tepid, 10 minutes.

COOK'S NOTE If the butter is added too quickly, the hollandaise may separate. Don't throw it away! Combine 1 tbsp water and 1 egg yolk in a clean bowl over a pan of simmering water set on a low heat. Make sure the base of the bowl is not in contact with the water. Whisk to a light and frothy mixture that holds that trail of the whisk, 3 minutes. Remove the pan from the heat. Whisk in the separated hollandaise, a little at a time, whisking vigorously after each addition, until the mixture re-emulsifies.

VARIATION To make plain hollandaise, replace lemon juice with 1½ tbsp white wine vinegar.

Sun-dried tomato and cannellini bean dip

Make this dip in advance and keep chilled, but serve it at room temperature. To add variety, use sun-blushed tomatoes instead of sun-dried ones.

Makes about 500ml (16fl oz)

Ingredients

400g tinned cannellini beans, drained
8 sun-dried tomatoes in oil, drained
1 garlic clove, chopped
1 tbsp chopped rosemary
4 tbsp olive oil
2 tbsp red wine vinegar
125ml (4fl oz) water
salt and freshly ground black pepper

1 Place the beans, sun-dried tomatoes, garlic, rosemary, oil, vinegar, and water in a food processor or blender; pulse to a smooth purée. If necessary, adjust the consistency by gradually adding more water, 1 tbsp at a time. Add salt and pepper to taste.

2 Cover and refrigerate for 30 minutes to allow the flavours to blend.

....

GET AHEAD Make dip up to 3 days in advance. Cover and refrigerate.

COOK'S NOTE Cannellini are slender, ivory white Italian beans. Their creamy texture and their ability to absorb strong, aromatic flavours makes them ideal for dips. If you cannot find a source for cannellini beans, any tinned white beans will make an excellent substitute.

Herbed yogurt dip

A fusion of fresh herbs mixed into creamy Greek yogurt acts as a wonderful dip for crudités, flat breads, and skewers of seared meat or fish.

Makes about 500ml (16fl oz)

Ingredients

15g (½oz) parsley, chopped
15g (½oz) basil, chopped
15g (½oz) chives, chopped
grated zest of ½ lemon
juice of 1 lemon
175g (6oz) cream cheese
250g (9oz) Greek-style yogurt
3 tbsp olive oil
salt and freshly ground black pepper

1 Place the herbs, lemon juice, cream cheese, yogurt, and oil in a food processor or blender; pulse until well blended. Add salt and pepper to taste.

2 Cover and refrigerate for 30 minutes to allow the flavours to blend. Serve chilled.

....

GET AHEAD Make dip up to 1 day in advance. Cover and refrigerate.

COOK'S NOTE Use your favourite bouquet of green herbs to flavour this fragrant dip. Choose from rocket, tarragon, marjoram, chervil, watercress, or lovage instead of one or all of our favourite combination of parsley, basil, and chives. For a lighter dip, use ricotta cheese in place of some or all of the cream cheese.

Salsa romesco dip

This piquant Spanish sauce will keep well for several days in the refrigerator. To add variety use different nuts.

Makes about 500ml (16fl oz)

Ingredients
1 red pepper, quartered and seeded
1 tbsp olive oil
75g (2½oz) almonds, skinned
5cm (2in) thick slice of day-old bread, cubed
2 garlic cloves, chopped
¼ tsp cayenne pepper
½ tsp paprika
15g (½oz) parsley, chopped
2 tomatoes, chopped
2 tbsp sherry vinegar
salt and freshly ground black pepper

1 Roast the pepper quarters skin side up under a hot grill until charred and wrinkled, 5–10 minutes. Place in a plastic bag or a bowl with a plate on top and leave until cool. The steam released by the peppers as they cool will loosen the skin.

2 Uncover cooled peppers. Peel off the charred skin using the tip of a small knife. Scrape rather than rinse off any remaining bits of skin. Rinsing the pepper will wash away the roasted flavour.

3 Heat oil in a pan over medium heat. Stir-fry the almonds and bread cubes until golden, 5 minutes. Drain on kitchen paper.

4 Place peeled pepper quarters, almonds, bread, garlic, spices, parsley, tomatoes, and vinegar in a food processor or blender; pulse until well blended but still retaining some texture. If necessary, adjust the consistency by gradually adding water 1 tbsp at a time. Add salt and pepper to taste.

5 Cover and refrigerate for 30 minutes to allow the flavours to blend. Serve chilled with dippers.

....

GET AHEAD Make dip up to 3 days in advance. Cover and refrigerate.

COOK'S NOTE You don't have to restrict yourself to using almonds in this piquant Catalan sauce. You can use hazelnuts, pine nuts, or a combination of either with the almonds, with equal authenticity.

Roast red pepper, feta, and mint dip

You can make this dip in advance, but serve at room temperature to enjoy the perfect blend of flavours.

Makes about 500ml (16fl oz)

Ingredients

3 red peppers, quartered and seeded
200g (7oz) feta cheese
200g (7oz) cream cheese
1 garlic clove, chopped
3 tbsp finely chopped fresh mint
2 tbsp olive oil
1 tbsp lemon juice
salt and freshly ground black pepper

1 Grill and peel the pepper quarters (see opposite, Steps 1 and 2).

2 Place peeled pepper quarters, feta, cream cheese, garlic, mint, oil, and lemon juice in a food processor or blender; pulse until well blended but still retaining some texture. If necessary, adjust consistency by gradually adding water 1 tbsp at a time. Add salt and pepper to taste.

3 Cover and refrigerate for 30 minutes to allow the flavours to blend. Serve with dippers.

....

GET AHEAD Make dip up to 3 days in advance. Cover and refrigerate.

Oven-dried root and fruit chips

These are very pretty and you can use them as a party snack or garnish. For an extra kick, try sprinkling them with smoked sweet paprika.

Makes 150g (5½oz)

Ingredients
1 small sweet potato, unpeeled
1 small beetroot, unpeeled
1 small parsnip, unpeeled
1 apple, unpeeled
1 pear, unpeeled
2 tsp salt

Essential equipment
either a food processor with
a slicing attachment,
a mandoline, or a Japanese
vegetable slicer

1 Preheat oven to 180°C (350°F/Gas 4).

2 Use either the slicing attachment on a food processor, mandoline, or Japanese vegetable slicer to slice the unpeeled sweet potato, beetroot, parsnip, apple, and pear 2mm (⅛in) thick. Place the slices in a single layer on oiled baking sheets. Put into oven.

3 Reduce oven temperature to 120°C (250°F/Gas ½). Bake for 1½ hours, turning the slices over every 20 minutes, until dried. Cool in single layers on wire racks. Sprinkle with salt. Serve at room temperature, with or without dips.

GET AHEAD Make up to 1 day in advance. Store in an airtight container at room temperature.

Crispy potato skins

This canapé will be popular with all your guests. Choose a couple of your favourite dips to serve with these moreish herb-coated potato skins.

Makes 40

Ingredients
5 medium potatoes, pricked
2 tbsp olive oil
1 tbsp finely chopped fresh rosemary or 2 tsp crumbled dried rosemary
1½ tsp salt and 1 tsp freshly ground black pepper

1 Preheat oven to 180°C (350°F/Gas 4).

2 Bake the potatoes until tender, 1 hour. Cool. Cut each potato into 6 wedges. Scoop out the cooked potato, leaving the skins intact and a shell of potato and skin, about 0.5cm (¼in) thick. If desired, reserve cooked potato for another use.

3 Brush potato skins with oil on both sides. Place in a single layer, scooped side up, on to a wire rack set on top of an oven tray. Sprinkle evenly with rosemary, and salt and pepper.

4 Bake for 15 minutes, then remove from oven and turn skins over. Return skins to the oven and continue baking until crisp and golden brown, 15 minutes. Serve at room temperature, with or without dips.

....

GET AHEAD Make up to 1 day in advance. Store in an airtight container at room temperature.

COOK'S NOTE Make this recipe the day before your party and use the reserved cooked potato to make a delicious potato mash for supper the night before.

Vegetable dippers

Arrange vegetables in an airtight container covered with damp kitchen paper. Cover and refrigerate. Serve chilled, with dips.

QUICK
& EASY

Prepare your chosen vegetables as directed below.

Baby carrots Choose firm, crisp baby carrots and use as quickly as possible. Do not peel. Trim root end, but leave a short green stem to act as a handle for dipping.

Baby potatoes Choose even-sized, small new potatoes with a crisp, waxy texture and papery, thin skins. Simmer, unpeeled, in salted water until tender when pierced with the tip of a small sharp knife. Use gold and red skinned potatoes for added colour contrast.

Carrots Avoid large carrots as they may have a tough, woody core. Cut into sticks about 8cm (3in) long and 0.5cm (¼in) thick.

Celery Use only the pale, tender inner stalks. The outer stalks tend to be stringy and should be peeled. Cut into sticks about 8cm (3in) long and 0.5cm (¼in) thick.

Chicory Trim the bitter stem end and use only the crisp, smaller inner leaves. Chicory is grown in red as well as white varieties.

Cherry tomatoes Try to find yellow as well as red for colour contrast. The plum and pear shaped cherry tomato varieties are now widely available. Their elongated shape makes them easier to use for dipping.

Cucumbers Scrape out the seeds and discard. Cut into sticks about 8cm (3in) long and 0.5cm (¼in) thick. Leave unpeeled for added colour contrast between the dark green peel and pearly pale green interior.

Radishes Trim the root end, but leave a little green stem on to act as a handle for dipping. Elongated French-style varieties with red tops and white tips are best for dipping.

GET AHEAD Prepare vegetables up to 1 day in advance.

COOK'S NOTE A generous quantity of just one or two vegetables makes an impressive display. Choose vegetables that are at their freshest, seasonal best, rather than aiming for a lavish selection.

Classic fish goujons

Everyone loves these crispy fried strips of white fish that can be served with so many different mayonnaise dips.

QUICK & EASY

Makes 20

Ingredients
225g (8oz) white fish fillets, skinned and boned
1 egg
45g (1½oz) fresh or panko breadcrumbs
pinch of salt
pinch of freshly ground black pepper or chilli powder
45g (1½oz) plain flour
2 litres (3½ pints) vegetable or sunflower oil
½ tsp sea salt to serve

Essential equipment
deep-fat fryer or deep-sided saucepan

1 Slice the fish fillets into 20 equal strips. Whisk the egg with 1 tablespoon water. Mix the breadcrumbs with salt and pepper or chilli powder.

2 Coat the fish in flour, then dip into the egg, coating evenly all over, and then roll in breadcrumbs. Lay on a tray and chill until needed.

3 To deep-fry, heat the oil in a deep-fat fryer or deep-sided saucepan to 190°C (375°F/Gas 5), or until a cube of bread browns in 30 seconds. Fry the goujons in 4 batches of 5 goujons at a time for 2 minutes, then drain on kitchen paper. Serve scattered with a little sea salt and home-made tartar sauce (see p88).

GET AHEAD These goujons freeze well uncooked in single layers. You can make them the day before serving.

COOK'S NOTE Recommended fish: try to use sustainably caught fish, such as cod, haddock, hake, sole, plaice, or other white fish or salmon.

VARIATION Use exactly the same method but with chicken breast instead. You can add 20g (¾oz) fresh Parmesan, grated or finely chopped parsley, and lemon zest to the breadcrumbs. Serve with flavoured mayonnaise.

Ginger hoisin chicken drummettes

Fresh ginger, hoisin, and soy sauce works so well with chicken, and baking them in this coating enhances its flavour.

Makes 20

Ingredients
20 chicken wings
10cm (4in) piece fresh
ginger, grated
2 garlic cloves, crushed
6 tbsp hoisin sauce
1 tbsp Chinese hot chilli sauce
1 tbsp light soy sauce
1 tbsp granulated sugar
1 tbsp water

Essential equipment
kitchen scissors or sharp
boning knife

1 For the drummettes, cut the first joint of each chicken wing and discard wing tips. Holding the small end of the second joint, cut, scrape, and push meat down to thick end. Pull skin and meat over end of bone with fingers to resemble baby drumsticks. Cut off knuckle end with scissors or knife. Repeat with remaining chicken wings.

2 Combine the ginger, garlic, sauces, sugar, and water in a non-metallic bowl. Add chicken and toss to coat each piece well. Cover and refrigerate for at least 1 hour.

3 Preheat oven to 180°C (350°F/Gas 4).

4 Place chicken on a wire rack set over an oven tray. Bake until chicken is well browned and cooked through, 35 minutes. Serve warm or at room temperature, with or without dips.

GET AHEAD Make drummettes up to 2 days in advance and marinate chicken up to 1 day in advance. Cover and refrigerate.

COOK'S NOTE The tips and first joint of chicken wings are basically just skin and bone. When making drummettes, reserve these parts for later use. They are ideal for making chicken stock.

Honey sesame-glazed cocktail sausages

Drizzling honey over roasting sausages glazes and sweetens the meat. Make double quantities as these sausages are extremely popular at parties.

Makes about 30

Ingredients
500g (1lb 2oz) cocktail sausages, separated
1 tbsp sesame seeds
½ tbsp runny honey

1 Preheat oven to 180°C (350°F/Gas 4).

2 Arrange the sausages in a single layer on an oiled oven tray. Bake for 20 minutes, then turn sausages over on the tray.

3 Roast until golden and cooked through, 15 minutes. Sprinkle with the sesame seeds and drizzle with honey. Toss to coat each sausage well. Serve hot or warm, with or without dips.

GET AHEAD Cook sausages up to 12 hours in advance. Cool and cover with foil. Reheat in 200°C (400°F/Gas 6) oven, 10 minutes. Alternatively, cook sausages up to 1 hour in advance. Cover with foil and keep warm. Toss with seeds and honey just before serving.

COOK'S NOTE Any good butcher that makes chipolata sausages will make cocktail sausages to order.

VARIATION
Honey rosemary glazed cocktail sausages Replace sesame seeds with 2 tsp finely chopped rosemary.

Sweet and spicy glazed cocktail sausages Replace honey and sesame seeds with 1½ tbsp mango chutney.

Sticky marmalade glazed cocktail sausages Replace honey and sesame seeds with 1 tbsp of fine rinded or rindless orange marmalade.

Sweet chilli glazed cocktail sausages Replace honey with 2 tbsp sweet chilli dipping sauce.

Chilled pea and avocado soup shot

Vibrant green and silky, this quick-to-make recipe celebrates the flavours of summer. Make on the day of the party.

QUICK & EASY

Makes 20 shot glasses

Ingredients
140g (5oz) frozen peas
2 ripe avocados halved, peeled, and stoned
4 spring onions, trimmed
4 tbsp lemon juice
10g (¼oz) fresh coriander
chilli powder to taste
600ml (1 pint) chicken stock, chilled
1 tbsp sour cream
salt and freshly ground black pepper

To garnish
50g (1¾oz) sour cream
2 tbsp finely chopped coriander

Essential equipment
shot glasses

1 Blanch the peas in boiling water for 2 minutes and drain.

2 Purée all the ingredients together in a food processor until smooth, and taste to check the seasoning.

3 Garnish with the sour cream and finely chopped coriander.

....

GET AHEAD Make on the same day as serving and chill until needed.

COOK'S NOTE Make with good-quality avocados.

Carrot, honey, and ginger soup cups

These little shots of hot, sweet, and spicy soup make fun and filling party fare, and are perfect for warming up your guests in winter.

Makes 20

Ingredients
30g (1oz) butter
750g (1lb 10oz) carrots, chopped
1 onion, chopped
1 garlic clove, chopped
10cm (4in) piece fresh ginger, chopped
3 celery sticks, chopped
salt and freshly ground black pepper
1 litre (1¾ pints) chicken stock
1 tbsp honey
4 tbsp double cream
1 tbsp chopped chives to garnish

Essential equipment
20 espresso, shot glasses, or demi-tasse cups

1 Melt the butter in a pan over low heat. Add the carrots, onion, garlic, ginger, and celery with a pinch of salt. Continue cooking, covered, until very soft, 20 minutes.

2 Add stock and increase heat to a boil. Reduce heat and simmer until carrots are cooked through, 15 minutes. Cool slightly, then place in a food processor or blender; pulse to a smooth purée.

3 Place a fine-mesh sieve over the rinsed out pan and push the purée through. Discard bits left behind. Add 1 tbsp water to the purée at a time to adjust the soup's thickness to a sipping consistency.

4 Heat soup through over medium heat. Add honey, cream, and salt and pepper to taste. Ladle into cups. Sprinkle with chives to garnish. Serve hot.

GET AHEAD Make up to 2 days in advance. Cover and refrigerate. This soup can also be frozen.

COOK'S NOTE Remember that this soup will be sipped from a cup and not served with a spoon. Add water as specified by the recipe to achieve the proper consistency for this.

Chilled spiced chickpea soup cups with avocado salsa

Summer fun in a glass, these simple chickpea shots are very simple to make, but are really tasty. You can make the soup two days ahead.

Makes 20

Ingredients

For the soup
400g tin of chickpeas, drained
400g tin of tomatoes
125ml (4fl oz) Greek-style yogurt
2 garlic cloves, crushed
1 tsp ground cumin
1 tbsp lemon juice
2 tbsp olive oil
salt
cayenne pepper

For the salsa
1 medium avocado
½ medium red onion, finely chopped
1 tbsp finely chopped mint
1 tbsp lemon juice
1 tbsp olive oil
salt and freshly ground black pepper
6 tbsp sour cream

Essential equipment
20 espresso, shot glasses, or demi-tasse cups

1 For the soup, place the chickpeas, tomatoes, yogurt, garlic, cumin, lemon juice, and oil in a food processor or blender; pulse to a smooth purée.

2 Transfer purée to a bowl. Gradually add up to 125ml (4fl oz) water to adjust the soup's thickness to a sipping consistency. Add salt and pepper to taste. Cover and refrigerate for 30 minutes to allow flavours to blend.

3 For the salsa, cut the avocado into fine dice.

4 Combine avocado, onion, mint, lemon juice, and oil. Add salt and pepper to taste. Cover and refrigerate for 15 minutes to allow flavours to blend.

5 Ladle soup into cups. Top with 1 tsp each of salsa and sour cream. Serve chilled.

....

GET AHEAD Make soup up to 2 days in advance. Cover and refrigerate. Make salsa up to 8 hours in advance. Cover tightly with cling film and refrigerate.

COOK'S NOTE To help keep the salsa from discolouring when making it in advance, press a piece of cling film directly on to the surface of the salsa. It's the oxygen in the air that turns peeled avocado brown, so the less air that comes into contact with the salsa, the longer it will look fresh.

crostini, croustades, and crisp tortillas

White bean and sage crostini

A great vegetarian stand-by, you can use basil instead of sage if you prefer. The topping is delicious served either on crostini or as a dip.

QUICK & EASY

Makes 20

Ingredients
3 tbsp olive oil
1 small onion, finely chopped
2 garlic cloves, finely chopped
4 sage leaves, finely chopped
400g tinned cannellini beans, drained
2 tbsp water
salt and freshly ground black pepper
20 crostini (see below)
1 ripe tomato, seeded and diced
extra olive oil for drizzling

1 Heat the oil in a saucepan. Add the onion, garlic, and sage. Cook over low heat until soft, about 5 minutes.

2 Add the beans, water, and salt and pepper to taste. Cook for about 10 minutes. Mash the beans with a wooden spoon to make a rough purée.

3 Spread bean purée on crostini. Top each crostini with a little diced tomato and a drizzle of olive oil. Serve warm or at room temperature.

GET AHEAD Make topping up to 3 days in advance. Cover and refrigerate. Return to room temperature before serving. Top crostini up to 1 hour before serving.

BASE RECIPE CROSTINI

Makes 20 | 20 slices day-old baguette, about 5–8cm (2–3in) in diameter; 4 tbsp olive oil.

Preheat oven to 180°C (350°F/Gas 4). Cut the baguette into 20 slices (1cm/½in thick) and place the slices on a baking sheet. Brush with the olive oil. Bake until crisp and lightly golden, 10 minutes. Leave to cool on a wire rack.

GET AHEAD Make crostini up to 2 weeks in advance. Cool completely and store in an airtight container.

COOK'S NOTE Add a crushed clove of garlic to the oil before brushing the bread for extra flavour.

Aubergine caviar crostini

QUICK & EASY

This is a great way to prepare aubergines to get their full flavour. It can also be used as a dip.

Makes 20

Ingredients
2 medium aubergines
1 garlic clove, crushed
juice of ½ lemon
2 tbsp olive oil
1 tbsp Greek-style yogurt
salt
cayenne pepper
20 crostini (see opposite)
20 mint sprigs
1 tsp paprika

1 Prick the aubergine several times with a fork. Grill it until skin is black and blistered, and the flesh feels soft. When cool enough to handle, peel off the charred skin. Place in a colander. Use hands to squeeze out as much moisture as possible from the flesh.

2 Place aubergine, garlic, lemon juice, oil, and yogurt in a food processor or blender; pulse to a smooth purée. Add salt and pepper to taste. Cool completely.

3 Spoon topping on to each crostini. Garnish with mint sprigs and a pinch of paprika. Serve at room temperature.

GET AHEAD Make topping up to 2 days in advance. Cover and refrigerate. Top crostini up to 45 minutes before serving.

6 ways with **crostini**

Little crostini make a perfect base for Mediterranean-style toppings. Contrast their crunchy texture with juicy, fresh ingredients. These recipes make 20.

goat's cheese and roasted cherry tomato crostini

Spread 150g (5½oz) soft goat's cheese on to one end of the crostini. Place a roasted cherry tomato (see above) on to the other end and tuck a mint leaf under the tomato. Season with black pepper to serve. For an alternative recipe that plays on the flavours of an Italian tricolore salad, replace the goat's cheese with a thin slice of buffalo mozzarella, and garnish with a fresh basil leaf. Top the crostini up to 30 minutes before serving.

citrus avocado purée crostini

Purée 1 large ripe avocado with 100g (3½oz) cream cheese, 1 garlic clove, 1 tbsp olive oil, grated zest of 1 lemon, juice of ½ lemon, salt, and Tabasco sauce to taste in a blender or food processor. Spoon on top of the crostini and garnish with finely chopped chives and a strip of lemon or zest or ½ a roasted cherry tomato (see above). You can replace the grated lemon zest and juice with lime and omit the Tabasco if you prefer.

sun-blushed tomato pesto crostini

Purée 140g (5oz) drained sun-blushed tomatoes with 1 garlic clove, 50g (1¾oz) toasted pine nuts, 2 tbsp olive oil, 45g (1½oz) grated Parmesan, 1 seeded red chilli, and 1 tbsp lemon juice in a blender or food processor. Check the seasoning and add more lemon juice if necessary. Carefully mound 1 tsp of pesto onto each crostini and garnish with a basil leaf. For a variation, garnish with very thin slices of basil and replace the sun-blushed tomatoes with sun-dried.

Know-how... roasting cherry tomatoes

Preheat oven to 180°C (350°F/ Gas 4). Place 10 cherry tomato halves on a baking tray, drizzle with oil, then scatter over sugar and salt and black pepper. Roast in the oven for 30 minutes, or until the tomatoes are dried out and very slightly caramelized.

GET AHEAD Tomatoes can be roasted, cooled, and chilled several days in advance.
VARIATIONS Fresh herbs, such as basil or thyme, and finely chopped garlic can also be scattered over the tomato halves before roasting.

pancetta and tomato with basil and almond pesto

Preheat oven to 180°C (350°F/Gas 4). Wrap 20 small cherry tomatoes in 10 slices of pancetta, sliced in half lengthways. Place on an oiled baking tray and bake for 20 minutes until the pancetta is cooked. Purée 1 bunch of basil with 2 tbsp olive oil, 1 garlic clove, 50g (1¾oz) roasted almonds, a squeeze of lemon, and salt and black pepper in a blender or food processor. Check the seasoning. Pile the pesto on top of each crostini and top with a roasted cherry tomato.

chargrilled aubergine with garlic and mint

Preheat a griddle. Slice 1 aubergine thinly then cut into half moons and toss in 1 tbsp olive oil. Mix together 1 tbsp olive oil, 1 finely chopped garlic clove, 1 tbsp chopped mint, ½ tbsp balsamic vinegar, and seasoning. Chargrill the aubergine on the griddle for 2 minutes on each side. Toss in the oil mixture and check the seasoning. Place 1 tsp of soft goat's cheese or ricotta on top of each crostini, top with the chargrilled aubergine, and garnish with mint.

fresh tomato salsa crostini

Mix together 4 ripe plum tomatoes, seeded and finely diced, with 2 tbsp finely chopped red onions, 2 tbsp olive oil, 1 finely chopped garlic clove, 1 tbsp balsamic vinegar, 2 tbsp very thinly sliced basil, and salt and black pepper. Spoon on top of each crostini and garnish with 2 fresh basil leaves.

For a variation, add 1 chopped, medium-ripe avocado with the tomatoes, replace the vinegar with 1 tbsp lemon juice, and use finely chopped coriander instead of basil. Garnish with coriander leaves.

Courgette and saffron bruschetta

These gorgeous little bruschettas have a herbaceous flavour. Adding lemon juice and zest brings out the tastes of summer.

QUICK & EASY

Makes 20

Ingredients
1 small baguette
olive oil
2 garlic cloves, peeled
2 courgettes
pinch of saffron threads
1 tbsp lemon juice, or to taste
salt and freshly ground
black pepper

To garnish
grated lemon zest
handful of basil or mint leaves

Essential equipment
griddle or grill

1 Preheat griddle or grill. Slice the baguette thinly on an angle, drizzle with olive oil, and grill until crisp on both sides.

2 Use 1 garlic clove to rub gently over the crisp bread.

3 Dice the courgettes and chop the other garlic clove finely. Heat a little oil in a pan and sauté courgette and garlic for 5 minutes.

4 Add a pinch of saffron and cook until vegetables start to turn golden. Add 1 tbsp lemon juice or more to taste, then season and use to top crisp bruschetta. Garnish with lemon zest and basil or mint leaves scattered over.

GET AHEAD The bruschetta can be made a few hours ahead.

COOK'S NOTE Make this when courgettes are in season as this recipe relies on the quality of the ingredients.

VARIATION Feta, goat's cheese, or ricotta can be added at the last minute to give a creamy rich contrast.

Step-by-step
Croustades

Thinly rolled out bread baskets baked until crisp make a versatile canapé base for so many fillings. They will become an irreplaceable part of your party repertoire.

Makes 20
Prep 5 minutes
Cook 10–15 minutes
Freezability You can freeze when cut but not baked

Ingredients
5 large slices of medium-thickness sliced white or brown bread
2 tbsp olive oil

Essential equipment
5cm (2in) round cookie cutter
24-hole mini muffin tin

GET AHEAD These can be made 1 week before and stored in an airtight container at room temperature.

COOK'S NOTE You can either bake these quickly as in the recipe, as long as you watch carefully, or you can bake in a low oven slowly to dry them out. When you remove the croustades from the oven they must be completely crisp throughout otherwise they will go stale once cooled.

VARIATION You can use white, brown, or flavoured breads as long as they are rolled out thinly. Melted butter can be used instead of olive oil.

1 Preheat oven to 180°C (350°F/Gas 4). Place the sliced bread on a chopping board and, using a sharp knife, cut off the crusts.

2 Using a rolling pin, press down heavily onto each slice of bread in turn to roll it out thinly, then set aside.

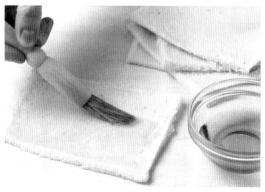

3 Using a pastry brush, brush each flattened bread slice all over with a little of the olive oil, then set aside. Make sure the bread is covered with the oil.

4 Use a cookie cutter to stamp out 4 rounds per slice. Bread slice sizes can differ so you may get more or less than 4 rounds.

7 Remove the croustades from the tin and allow to cool on a wire rack. At this stage you can store them in an airtight container.

5 Push each bread round carefully into the holes of a mini muffin tin, pressing down evenly so the croustades will be flat-bottomed.

6 Bake in the oven for 10 minutes, or until the croustades are lightly coloured and crisp, then remove the tin from the oven.

Fill the croustades with your chosen filling 45 minutes before serving and watch them fly off the table! Find this filling on pp118–19.

Poached salmon with dill mayonnaise croustades

Salmon and fresh dill are a perfect combination, and these delicious canapés will become a perennial favourite in your repertoire.

QUICK & EASY

Makes 20

Ingredients
300g (10oz) salmon fillet
20 croustades (see pp114–5)
salt
white pepper
6 tbsp mayonnaise (see p88)
2 tbsp finely chopped dill

To garnish
20 dill sprigs
grated lemon zest

1 Place the salmon in pan of boiling water. When water returns to boil, remove from heat at once and leave to cool completely.

2 Drain salmon on kitchen paper. Separate into large flakes. Divide salmon among croustades. Sprinkle with salt and pepper.

3 Combine the mayonnaise and dill. Spoon mayonnaise over salmon. Garnish with dill sprigs and lemon zest. Serve at room temperature.

....

GET AHEAD Cook salmon the day before. Make mayonnaise up to 2 days in advance. Cover and refrigerate. Fill croustades up to 45 minutes before serving.

COOK'S NOTE Use very finely chopped coriander and a squeeze of lime in place of dill to create a subtle oriental flavour.

Chicken tonnato with lemon and capers croustades

QUICK & EASY

This is a slant on a popular Italian summer classic. Prepare the sauce and chicken in advance if required, but assemble just before the party.

Makes 20

Ingredients
1 boneless, skinless chicken breast
2 tbsp drained tuna
2 drained anchovy fillets
2 tbsp mayonnaise (see p88)
1 tsp lemon juice
salt and freshly ground black pepper
20 croustades (see pp114–5)
20 drained capers
zest of ½ lemon to garnish

Essential equipment
zester

1 Put the chicken in a pan and cover with cold water. Bring slowly to a simmer over medium-low heat. Simmer gently without boiling until cooked through, 7–10 minutes.

2 Cool completely in cooking liquid. Drain and slice chicken into fine strips.

3 For the sauce, place the tuna, anchovies, mayonnaise, and lemon juice in a food processor; pulse until smooth. Add salt and pepper to taste.

4 Divide chicken among croustades. Spoon over sauce. Garnish with capers and lemon zest. Serve at room temperature.

GET AHEAD Make tonnato sauce up to 3 days in advance. Cover and refrigerate. Cook chicken up to 1 day in advance. Cover and refrigerate. Fill croustades up to 45 minutes before serving.

Quail egg and crispy bacon croustades

These attractive croustades are perfect for any special occasion. To save time, cook the eggs two days ahead and then assemble on the day.

Makes 20

Ingredients
10 quail eggs
6 tbsp mayonnaise (see p88)
20 croustades (see pp114–5)
6 rashers crispy bacon, sliced
snipped chives or chervil
to garnish

1 Cook the quail eggs in a pan of boiling water for 2½ minutes. Drain and refresh in cold water. Peel and cut in half.

2 Spoon the mayonnaise into the croustades. Place half a quail egg on an angle, cut side up, on top of the mayonnaise. Top with the sliced bacon and garnish with the snipped chives or chervil. Serve at room temperature.

GET AHEAD Cook and peel the eggs up to 2 days in advance. Cover with water and refrigerate. Fill the croustades up to 45 minutes before serving.

COOK'S NOTE As an alternative filling, try with mayonnaise (see p88), black and red lumpfish caviar, and chervil or parsley sprigs

Tomato concasse with crème fraîche and chive croustades

A treat for vegetarians, ensure you use ripe tomatoes for this simple but stunning combination with crème fraîche and chives.

Makes 20

Ingredients

3 ripe tomatoes, peeled, seeded, and diced
2 tbsp finely chopped chives
2 tbsp crème fraîche
2 tbsp lemon juice
Tabasco sauce
salt and freshly ground black pepper
20 croustades (see pp114–5)

1 For the concasse, combine the tomatoes with chives, crème fraîche, lemon juice, and a dash of Tabasco. Cover and refrigerate for 1 hour. Add salt and pepper to taste.

2 Spoon concasse into croustades. Serve cold.

GET AHEAD Make concasse the day before, but add salt and pepper just before using. Store in an airtight container in the refrigerator. Fill croustades up to 45 minutes before serving.

VARIATION You could replace chives with the same quantity of chopped tarragon or basil.

Mini Caesar salad croustades

A Caesar salad in one mouthful, these mini bread baskets provide a modern twist on the croûtons in the classic recipe.

QUICK & EASY

Makes 20

Ingredients
2 romaine hearts,
leaves separated
2 tbsp mayonnaise
(see p88)
dash of Worcestershire sauce
squeeze of lemon juice
5 drained anchovy fillets,
finely chopped
1 tbsp grated Parmesan cheese
20 croustades (see pp114–5)
20 Parmesan shavings
to garnish

1 Stack the salad leaves and roll up tightly. Slice across roll to make 0.5cm (¼in) strips.

2 Flavour mayonnaise with Worcestershire sauce and lemon juice.

3 Toss salad with mayonnaise, anchovies, and grated Parmesan.

4 Fill the croustades with salad. Garnish with Parmesan shavings.

GET AHEAD Prepare salad leaves up to 1 day in advance. Store in an airtight container in the refrigerator. Fill croustades up to 1 hour before serving.

Crisp tortillas with blackened snapper, peach relish, and sour cream

Seared spiced snapper with citrus fruit relish makes a surprisingly irresistible and elegant canapé. Any delicate white fish could work well.

QUICK & EASY

Makes 24

Ingredients

¼ tsp dried thyme
¼ tsp dried oregano
¼ tsp paprika
¼ tsp cumin seeds
¼ tsp garlic powder
½ tsp salt and ¼ tsp freshly ground black pepper
125g (4½oz) red snapper fillet, 1cm (½in) thick
2 tsp sunflower oil
1 stoned peach, fresh or tinned, finely diced
2 tsp lemon juice
24 crisp tortillas (see below)
5 tbsp sour cream to garnish

1 Combine the thyme, oregano, paprika, cumin, garlic, and salt and pepper on a plate. Cut the fish into 24 cubes (1cm/½in). Dip fish first in oil, then roll in spice mixture.

2 Preheat a dry frying pan over medium heat until very hot. Add fish cubes. Cook cubes 2 minutes per side until firm to the touch. Remove from pan and cool.

3 For the relish, combine the peach and lemon juice. Divide relish evenly among crisp tortillas. Top with fish. Garnish with sour cream. Serve chilled or at room temperature.

GET AHEAD Cook fish up to 1 day in advance. Cover and refrigerate. Make relish up to 1 day in advance. Cover and refrigerate. Top crisp tortillas up to 45 minutes before serving.

CRISP TORTILLAS

Makes 24 | 3 flour tortillas (15cm/6in); ½ tbsp sunflower oil; ¼ tsp salt

Preheat oven to 200°C (400°F/Gas 6). Brush tortillas on one side with oil. Cut each tortilla into 8 even-sized wedges with kitchen scissors or a serrated knife. Arrange oiled side up in a single layer on an oiled baking sheet. Sprinkle with salt. Bake until crisp, 5–7 minutes. Cool on a wire rack.

GET AHEAD Make crisp tortillas up to 5 days in advance. Store in an airtight container at room temperature.

COOK'S NOTE Good quality bought corn chips can be used as a time-saving alternative. Be sure to buy plain, lightly salted chips, not ones that are flavoured with spices.

Crisp tortillas with citrus ceviche

Use really fresh fish for this marinade, which can be tossed with the salad ingredients at the last minute. The tortillas can be made well in advance.

Makes 24

Ingredients
125g (4½oz) halibut fillet
juice of 1 lime
juice of ½ lemon
2 tbsp orange juice
1 red chilli, seeded
and finely chopped
1 spring onion, white stem
only, finely chopped
1 tomato, seeded and diced
1 small avocado, diced
2 tbsp finely chopped coriander
½ tsp salt
24 crisp tortillas (see opposite)

1 Finely dice the fish. Combine fish with the lime, lemon, and orange juices in a non-metallic bowl. Cover and refrigerate for 3 hours, stirring occasionally.

2 Drain fish well, discarding all but 1 tbsp marinade. Toss the fish, chilli, spring onion, tomato, avocado, coriander, salt, and reserved 1 tbsp marinade together to combine.

3 Top crisp tortillas with equal amounts of the ceviche. Serve chilled.

GET AHEAD Make ceviche up to 1 day in advance, but do not add the avocado, salt, and coriander more than 3 hours before serving. Press cling film tightly over the surface of the ceviche and refrigerate. Top crisp tortillas just before serving.

COOK'S NOTE Fresh tuna, salmon, or scallops also make excellent ceviche. Use cooked prawns if you prefer not to use raw fish.

Seared sesame tuna with wasabi-avocado on tortilla crisps

Full of Far Eastern flavours, the combination of bright green, peppery avocado and seared sesame tuna on a crisp tortilla works like a dream.

QUICK & EASY

Makes 24

Ingredients
2 tortilla wraps (25cm/10in)
2 tbsp olive oil
sea salt
2 ripe avocados, halved, peeled, and stoned
2 tbsp lime juice
pinch of salt
1 tsp wasabi paste
4 spring onions, finely chopped
150g (5½oz) tuna loin
30g (1oz) sesame seeds
1 tbsp sunflower oil
coriander leaves to garnish

Essential equipment
non-stick baking tray
non-stick frying pan

1 Preheat oven to 140°C (275°F/Gas 1).

2 Brush the tortilla wraps with olive oil and scatter with sea salt. Slice each tortilla into 12 triangles or stamp out into rounds with a cookie cutter. Place onto a non-stick baking tray and bake for 15 minutes, or until crisp.

3 Finely chop the avocado or mash with lime juice, salt, wasabi, and spring onions, then taste to check seasoning.

4 Slice the tuna into 4 square strips (1cm/½in) and roll in sesame seeds.

5 Preheat the frying pan with the sunflower oil and when very hot, flash fry tuna strips for 30 seconds on each side quickly. Cover and refrigerate until needed.

6 Slice each strip of tuna into 6 equal pieces to make a total of 24 pieces. To assemble, top each tortilla crisp with ½ tsp of wasabi-avocado, a slice of tuna, and fresh coriander leaves.

....

GET AHEAD The crisps can be made 1 week ahead and stored in an airtight container. The tuna can be prepared 1 day ahead, covered, and chilled, slice when serving. The wasabi-avocado can be made 8 hours before, cover well. Top 1 hour before serving.

COOK'S NOTE All avocados differ in size and flavour so you may need to add more wasabi, lime, and salt depending on your taste. Make sure the avocado is well covered with cling film, allowing no air in so as not to discolour.

VARIATION Replace wasabi with coriander and green chilli. Pickled ginger is a good garnish.

Sun-blushed tomato anchoïade on tortilla crisps

This punchy tomato and anchovy paste works beautifully served on a crisp tortilla. Use basil instead of parsley, if you prefer.

Makes 24

Ingredients
1 tbsp olive oil
1 small garlic clove, chopped
pinch of sea salt
2 tortilla wraps (4cm/10in)

For the anchoïade
6 anchovy fillets
2 tbsp milk
1 garlic clove, peeled
140g sun-blushed tomatoes, drained
2 tbsp extra virgin olive oil
1 tsp capers, washed and drained
15g (½oz) flat-leaf parsley

To garnish
100g (3½oz) goat's or cream cheese
6 black olives, pitted and cut into quarters

1 Preheat oven to 180°C (350°F/Gas 4).

2 Mix the oil, garlic, and salt together and use to brush the wraps. Slice or cut wraps into 24 triangles or rounds, lay on a baking tray, and bake until golden and completely dry and crisp, 8–10 minutes. Remove from oven, cool, and store.

3 For the anchoïade, put the anchovies in the milk and soak for 10 minutes to remove some of the saltiness, then drain and dry the anchovies on kitchen paper.

4 Put the anchovies, garlic, sun-blushed tomatoes, oil, capers, and parsley into a food processor; pulse until well combined. Taste to check the seasoning.

5 To serve, put some anchoïade on the tortilla crisp and top with a little goat's cheese and quarter of an olive.

GET AHEAD The tortilla crisps can be made several days ahead and stored in an airtight container. The anchoïade can be made 3 days ahead, covered and chilled.

COOK'S NOTE The tortilla crisps can be cut into any shape or even strips and used for dips. They must be crisp throughout when they come out of the oven otherwise they will go stale once they are cooled.

VARIATION Chopped herbs can be added to the flavoured oil.

quesadillas and pizzettes

Shredded spiced pork quesadilla with sour cream

This is traditional Mexican fare – roast pork fillet in a spicy tomato sauce with cheese and herbs – and it packs quite a punch!

Makes 24

Ingredients
2½ tbsp olive oil
200g (7oz) pork fillet
1 small onion, finely chopped
2 garlic cloves, finely chopped
½ tsp ground cumin
1 red chilli, seeded
and finely chopped
400g tin tomatoes, drained
salt and freshly ground
black pepper
4 tortilla wraps (18cm/7in)
2 tbsp finely chopped
fresh flat-leaf parsley
1 tbsp finely chopped fresh
oregano leaves
2 spring onions, finely chopped
100g (3½oz) Cheddar
cheese, grated
60g (2oz) sour cream
1 recipe salsa cruda
(see opposite)

Essential equipment
small non-stick frying pan
medium non-stick frying pan

1 Preheat oven to 180°C (350°F/Gas 4).

2 Heat ½ tbsp of oil in a small frying pan. Sear the fillet all over, then roast in the oven for 20 minutes.

3 Using the same frying pan as the pork, sauté the onion, garlic, cumin, and chilli in 1 tbsp oil until soft, then add the drained tomato, and stir well to break up the tomato. Cook for about 20 minutes over low heat until thickened and reduced.

4 Shred the pork thinly into the tomato sauce and adjust the seasoning. Cool. Spread the pork over 2 tortillas, scatter over the herbs and spring onions. Top with the grated cheese and sandwich together with the remaining 2 tortillas.

5 Heat a medium frying pan with 1 tbsp oil and sear the quesadillas for 1 minute on each side to brown, then transfer to a non-stick baking sheet and bake in oven, 5 minutes. Serve each quesadilla sliced into 12 triangles with sour cream and salsa cruda (see opposite).

GET AHEAD The pork mixture can be frozen or made several days ahead and refrigerated. The quesadillas can be assembled 1 day ahead and fried when ready to serve.

COOK'S NOTE Use whole tinned tomatoes as they are the best quality. Adjust the spices in the sauce according to your taste.

VARIATION Chicken can replace the pork and coriander can replace the parsley.

Goat's cheese and caramelized red onion quesadillas with salsa cruda

These tasty quesadillas will be popular with both vegetarians and meat-eaters. Make the quesadillas the day before, if preferred.

Makes 24

Ingredients

3 tbsp olive oil
2 red onions, thinly sliced
salt and freshly ground black pepper
1 tbsp red wine vinegar
1 tsp soft brown sugar
100g (3½oz) soft goat's cheese
4 tortilla wraps (18cm/7in)
1 small bunch of basil

For the salsa cruda

1 tomato, skinned, seeded, and chopped
½ red onion, finely chopped
10g (¼oz) coriander, chopped
1 green chilli, seeded and finely chopped
1 tbsp lemon juice
salt
2 tbsp extra virgin olive oil

Essential equipment

medium non-stick frying pan

1 Heat 2 tbsp of the oil in a small saucepan and sauté the red onions until wilted. Add a pinch of salt and the vinegar and cook over low heat, stirring occasionally, 5 minutes. Add the sugar and continue to cook gently for 10 minutes, until caramelized and soft.

2 Spread the goat's cheese over 2 of the tortillas, then spread the onions on top. Scatter the basil leaves and pepper over and top with remaining tortillas. Cover and chill until needed. Meanwhile, mix all the salsa cruda ingredients together and taste to check the seasoning.

3 Preheat oven to 180°C (350°F/Gas 4).

4 Preheat the frying pan with remaining oil. Fry tortilla on each side for 1 minute to brown then transfer to a non-stick baking sheet and bake in oven, 5 minutes. Slice tortilla into 12 triangles and serve with salsa cruda.

....

GET AHEAD The quesadillas can be made the day before, fry to serve. They can be kept warm in a medium-low oven for 30 minutes.

COOK'S NOTE Using a 18cm (7in) tortilla makes them canapé size once cut, but you can use larger tortillas.

VARIATION Replace the red onions with white, and red wine vinegar with balsamic vinegar. Replace the basil with oregano leaves.

Classic cheese quesadilla with green chilli, coriander, and avocado salsa

These are simple, versatile, and fun party or picnic food.
Serve with fresh salsas, avocados, limes, and tomatoes.

QUICK & EASY

Makes 24

Ingredients

For the salsa
2 ripe avocados
½ red onion, very finely chopped
½ red chilli, seeded and chopped
juice of 1 lime
salt and freshly ground black pepper
1 tbsp olive oil
dash of Tabasco sauce, or to taste

For the quesadilla
4 flour tortillas (18cm/7in)
175g (6oz) grated Swiss Gruyère cheese
30g (1oz) coriander, finely chopped
1 bunch of spring onions, trimmed and finely chopped
1 green chilli, seeded and finely chopped
salt and freshly ground black pepper
olive oil

Essential equipment
large non-stick frying pan
fish slice or palette knife

1 For the salsa, skin and stone the avocado. Finely chop or mash the avocado with the remaining ingredients and taste for seasoning.

2 Place 2 tortillas on the work surface. Divide the cheese, coriander, spring onions, chilli, and salt and pepper evenly between them. Press the 2 remaining tortillas on top to make a sandwich.

3 Heat a large frying pan with a drizzle of oil. Sear tortilla sandwiches over medium heat, 2–3 minutes on each side, or until light golden in colour and crisp. Flip with a fish slice or a palette knife.

4 Cut each quesadilla into 12 wedges and serve with avocado salsa.

....

GET AHEAD The quesadillas can be made several days ahead, covered, and kept in the refrigerator until you need them. You can fry them and keep warm in a low oven to serve to your guests.

Quesadilla triangles with hot pepper relish

With the addition of spiced peppers, this is the ultimate Mexican grilled cheese sandwich. Make up to one hour in advance.

QUICK & EASY

Makes 24

Ingredients

6 flour tortillas (15cm/6in)
1 tbsp sunflower oil
1 red pepper, quartered and seeded
2 green chillies, seeded and finely diced
½ garlic clove, crushed
1 tbsp olive oil
1 tbsp red wine vinegar
2 tbsp finely chopped coriander
¼ tsp granulated sugar
salt and freshly ground black pepper
6 tbsp grated Gruyère cheese
1 spring onion to garnish
75ml (2½fl oz) sour cream

Essential equipment

cast-iron grill pan

1 Preheat a grill pan over medium heat.

2 Brush 1 side of a tortilla with oil. Place tortilla oiled side down on to the pan, pressing lightly with a spatula. Cook until just marked, 1 minute. Repeat with remaining tortillas.

3 For relish, grill and peel the pepper quarters (see p92, Steps 1 and 2). Finely chop grilled pepper. Combine pepper with the chilli, garlic, oil, vinegar, coriander, and sugar. Add salt and pepper to taste. Cover and leave to stand for 1 hour at room temperature to allow the flavours to blend.

4 Preheat oven to 200°C (400°F/Gas 6).

5 Place half the tortillas on a baking sheet. Sprinkle 1 tbsp cheese, then spread 1 tbsp relish over each tortilla. Sprinkle another 1 tbsp cheese over each tortilla. Top with remaining tortillas. Bake until cheese melts, 5 minutes. Cool slightly.

6 Cut spring onion diagonally into 1cm (½in) pieces. Cut each quesadilla into 8 wedges with kitchen scissors or a serrated knife.

7 For the garnish, top quesadilla triangles with sour cream and a piece of spring onion. Serve warm or at room temperature.

....

GET AHEAD Make relish up to 1 day in advance. Cover and refrigerate. Prepare tortillas and fill up to 1 hour before serving. Cover and keep at room temperature.

COOK'S NOTE We recommend wearing rubber gloves when working with chillies. Capsaicin, the substance in chillies that makes them hot and spicy, can cause a painful burning sensation if brought into contact with eyes or sensitive skin.

Quesadilla triangles with smoky shredded chicken

QUICK & EASY

A warm heat infuses the chicken through this rich, flavourful sauce. These mini Mexican tortillas are best served warm or at room temperature.

Makes 24

Ingredients
1 boneless, skinless chicken breast
3 tbsp sunflower oil
½ medium onion, finely chopped
2 garlic cloves, crushed
½ tsp ground cumin
½ tsp ground coriander
1 tinned chipotle pepper in adobo sauce, chopped
1 tin of chopped tomatoes (200g)
1 tsp tomato purée
½ tsp sugar
salt and freshly ground black pepper
6 flour tortillas (15cm/6in)
6 tbsp grated Gruyère cheese
2 spring onions, finely chopped
75ml (2½fl oz) sour cream
24 coriander leaves to garnish

Essential equipment
cast-iron grill pan

1 Place the chicken in a pan and cover it with cold water. Bring to a simmer over low heat. Simmer gently without boiling until cooked through, 7–10 minutes. Cool completely before draining. Drain and shred chicken.

2 Heat 2 tbsp oil in a skillet over medium heat. Stir-fry the onion until softened, 5 minutes. Add the garlic, cumin, coriander, chipotle, tomato, tomato purée, and sugar. Cook until thickened, 5 minutes. Leave to cool. Combine with shredded chicken. Add salt and pepper to taste.

3 Preheat a grill pan over medium heat. Brush 1 side of a tortilla with oil. Place oiled side down on to the pan, pressing lightly with a spatula. Cook until just marked, 1 minute. Repeat with remaining tortillas.

4 Preheat oven to 200°C (400°F/Gas 6).

5 Place half the tortillas on a baking sheet marked side down. Combine cheese and spring onions. Sprinkle 1 tbsp cheese-onion mix, then 1 tbsp chicken on top of the cheese. Sprinkle another 1 tbsp cheese-onion mix over the chicken. Top with remaining tortillas.

6 Bake until cheese melts, 5 minutes. Cool slightly. Cut into 8 wedges with kitchen scissors or a serrated knife. Garnish triangles with sour cream and coriander leaves. Serve warm or at room temperature.

GET AHEAD Make chicken up to 1 day in advance. Cover and refrigerate. Prepare tortillas and fill up to 1 hour before serving. Cover and keep at room temperature.

Step-by-step Pizzette bases

This basic bread dough recipe will make the perfect mini pizzettes. Vary the toppings to suit the occasion and season. The dough can be made a day ahead.

Makes 20
Prep 25 minutes, plus 1½ hours rising
Cook 10–15 minutes
Freezability You can freeze the uncooked bases on sheets of greaseproof paper

Ingredients
250g (9oz) strong white flour
1 tsp salt
165ml (5½fl oz) warm water
1 tsp olive oil
1 tsp fast-action dried yeast

Essential equipment
5cm (2in) round cookie cutter

GET AHEAD Make the dough the day before, cover, and refrigerate overnight to rise. Leave at room temperature for 30 minutes before rolling out to use.

COOK'S NOTE The amount of liquid required can vary according to the flour used and the temperature outside. Add extra water 1 tbsp at a time as required. It is better to make the dough too soft than too dry.

VARIATION Add 1 tbsp chopped rosemary, thyme, or olives to the flour before adding the liquid. You can use this dough for flat bread, sprinkling with chopped garlic, grated Parmesan, and fresh herbs.

1 Place the flour and salt in a large mixing bowl and make a well in the centre of the flour. Pour the water and oil into the well.

2 Sprinkle the yeast over the liquid in the well and leave for 5 minutes. Using a wooden spoon, draw the flour into the middle and mix to form a sticky dough.

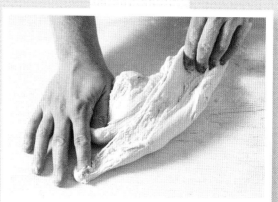

3 Knead the dough on a floured surface into a round. Use the heel of your hand to push the dough away and with the other hand turn the dough towards you.

4 Repeat this kneading action for 10 minutes until a smooth, shiny, and elastic dough is formed. Place the dough in a lightly oiled bowl and cover.

5 Leave the dough to rise in a warm place for 1½ hours. Deflate the dough by pressing down with your hand. The dough is now ready to be used.

6 Preheat oven to 180°C (350°F/Gas 4). Roll the dough out on a lightly floured surface to about 1cm (½in) thick. It should be even all over.

7 Using a cookie cutter, cut out little rounds and place onto a baking tray lined with greaseproof paper or a lightly oiled baking tray.

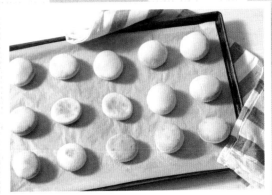

8 Bake in the oven for 10–15 minutes until lightly browned, or at this stage you can top with your chosen toppings.

Preferably while they are still warm, load up your pizzette bases with toppings and then watch them go like hot cakes! Find this topping on p139.

Tomato and basil pizzette

A simple but classic pizzette, this mini pizza will be a firm favourite.
Try adding little cubes of goat's cheese instead of the mozzarella.

Makes 20

Ingredients
1 recipe unbaked bread dough
(see pp134–5)
125g (4½oz) mozzarella
cheese, finely sliced
125ml (4fl oz) tomato passata
15g (½oz) small basil leaves
4 tbsp grated Parmesan cheese
salt and freshly ground
black pepper

Essential equipment
5cm (2in) plain cookie cutter

1 Preheat oven to 200°C (400°F/Gas 6).

2 Roll out the dough on a floured surface to a 0.25cm (⅛in) thickness. Stamp out 20 rounds with the cookie cutter and place on a floured baking sheet.

3 Cut the mozzarella slices into 20 equal-sized pieces. Spread each round with 1 tsp tomato passata and arrange over 2 basil leaves. Place a piece of mozzarella on top.

4 Sprinkle with Parmesan, and salt and pepper. Bake until crisp and golden, 10 minutes. Serve warm.

GET AHEAD Make up to 1 day in advance. Cover and refrigerate. Crisp in preheated 200°C (400°F/Gas 6) oven for 10 minutes before serving.

Aubergine and pine nut pizzette

Sautéed aubergines with pine nuts make a tempting pizzette topping. A sprinkling of basil just before serving is a lovely addition.

Makes 20

Ingredients
1 recipe unbaked bread dough
(see pp134–5)
1 medium aubergine
1 tbsp olive oil
1 garlic clove, rushed
2 tbsp finely chopped parsley
125ml (4fl oz) tomato passata
4 tbsp grated Parmesan cheese
3 tbsp pine nuts
salt and freshly ground
black pepper

Essential equipment
5cm (2in) plain cookie cutter

1 Preheat oven to 200°C (400°F/Gas 6).

2 Roll out the dough on a floured surface to a 0.25cm (⅛in) thickness. Stamp out 20 rounds with the cookie cutter and place on a floured baking sheet.

3 Cut the aubergine in half lengthways, then cut halves into 0.5cm (¼in) thick slices.

4 Heat oil in a frying pan and add aubergine, garlic, and parsley. Stir-fry over high heat until wilted, 5 minutes. Spread each pizzette with 1 tsp tomato passata. Arrange aubergine slices on top.

5 Sprinkle with Parmesan, pine nuts, and salt and pepper. Bake until crisp and golden, 10 minutes. Serve warm.

....

GET AHEAD Make up to 1 day in advance. Cover and refrigerate. Crisp in preheated 200°C (400°F/Gas 6) oven for 10 minutes before serving.

Mini beef burger with chilli jam and marinated beetroot pizzettes

This mini classic is always a favourite when made well with this zingy and colourful combination of chilli jam and fresh beetroot.

Makes 25

Ingredients
450g (1lb) beef mince
100g (3½oz) fresh breadcrumbs
2 garlic cloves, crushed
2 tbsp finely chopped onion
1 tsp Worcestershire sauce
1 tsp Dijon mustard
1 egg
salt and freshly ground
black pepper
1 beetroot, peeled and
finely grated
1 tsp red wine vinegar
1 tbsp olive oil or sunflower oil
450g (1lb) chilli jam (see p47)
25 pizzette bases (see pp134–5)
thyme leaves to garnish

1 Mix the mince, breadcrumbs, garlic, onion, Worcestershire sauce, mustard, egg, and seasoning together well.

2 Divide into 25 balls and, using damp hands, shape into mini burgers. Chill until ready to cook.

3 Mix the grated beetroot with vinegar, and season with salt.

4 Preheat a frying pan with the oil. Sear the mini burgers, uncrowded, in a pan for 1½ minutes on each side, slightly flattening with a spatula as you turn them.

5 To serve, place ½ tsp of chilli jam on each pizzette base, add a mini burger and top with a small mound of the marinated beetroot. Garnish with thyme to serve.

....

GET AHEAD The burgers can be made a day ahead or frozen.

COOK'S NOTE Mix burger ingredients together gently, as heavy handling or pounding will make burgers tough and heavy to eat.

VARIATION Use minced lamb instead of beef and a finely chopped red chilli can be added to the mixture. Replace beetroot with finely grated Cheddar cheese.

Rosemary flat bread with garlic, Parmesan, and olives

A variation on pizzette dough (see pp134–5), this makes a versatile flat bread. It is excellent served with dips and will be a popular choice.

Makes 1 (23cm x 30cm/ 9in x 12in) flat bread

Ingredients
250g (9oz) strong white flour
1 tsp salt
2 tbsp chopped fresh rosemary leaves
½ tsp caster sugar
150ml (5fl oz) warm water
1 tsp olive oil
1 tsp fast-action dried yeast
1 tbsp polenta
1 tbsp grated Parmesan cheese

For the topping
1 tbsp olive oil
1 garlic clove, finely chopped
20 black olives, pitted and sliced
15g (½oz) Parmesan, grated
sea salt

1 Place the flour, salt, rosemary, and sugar in a medium bowl and make a well in the centre. Pour in the warm water and oil. Sprinkle the yeast over the liquid, give the liquid a little stir, and leave for 5 minutes.

2 Draw the dry ingredients into the liquid with a blunt table knife and mix into rough dough. Turn dough out on a lightly floured surface and knead until smooth, shiny, and elastic, 10 minutes.

3 Place dough in a lightly oiled bowl, cover with a tea towel, and leave to rise for 1½ hours.

4 Preheat oven to 200°C (400°F/Gas 6).

5 Deflate dough with your hand and turn out onto a lightly floured surface. Roll dough out to 23cm x 30cm (9in x 12in). Sprinkle the polenta and Parmesan onto a baking tray and place flat bread on top.

6 For the topping, mix the oil with garlic and drizzle or brush over the bread. Scatter over the olives, Parmesan, and sea salt and bake until crisp, 10–15 minutes. Transfer to a wire rack. Slice into thin strips to serve with dips.

....

GET AHEAD The dough can be made the day before and left in the refrigerator to rise overnight. The flat breads can be baked hours ahead and reheated to serve.

COOK'S NOTE All ovens vary so it may take a few minutes more or less than the suggested timing. The base of polenta and Parmesan gives flavour and helps crispen the base.

VARIATION Chopped olives can be used in place of the rosemary or any other herb. Toppings can vary: try anchovy, chillies, blue cheese, sun-dried tomatoes, sliced artichokes, or pecorino cheese.

Mini pissaladière

A speciality from southern France, these mini tarts will still taste great if you decide to leave out the anchovies. They are ideal for a summer party.

Makes 24

Ingredients
1 recipe unbaked shortcrust pastry (see pp172–3)
1 tbsp olive oil
1 garlic clove, crushed
2 large Spanish onions, finely sliced
200ml (7fl oz) tomato passata
1 tsp dried oregano
salt and freshly ground black pepper
1 tbsp grated Parmesan cheese
6 anchovies, halved lengthways
24 pitted black olives

Essential equipment
35cm x 25cm (14in x 10in) Swiss roll pan

1 Preheat oven to 200°C (400°F/Gas 6).

2 Roll out the pastry on a floured surface to fit pan. Place rolled pastry in the oiled pan.

3 Heat the oil in a frying pan over medium heat. Add the garlic and onion and cook until soft, 10 minutes. Add the tomato passata and continue cooking for 5 minutes. Add the oregano, and salt and pepper to taste.

4 Spread the onion mixture evenly over the pastry. Bake for 15 minutes. Remove from the oven and sprinkle with Parmesan. Allow to cool in the pan, then cut into 24 squares (5cm x 5cm/ 2in x 2in).

5 Cut the anchovy pieces in half lengthways. Top each square with 2 anchovy pieces in a criss-cross pattern with an olive in the centre. Remove from pan and serve at room temperature.

GET AHEAD Make, cut, and garnish, but leave in pan, up to 2 days in advance. Store in pan, covered, in the refrigerator. Crisp in preheated 200°C (400°F/Gas 6) oven for 10 minutes. Remove from pan before serving.

röstis, fritters, and pancakes

Step-by-step
Potato rösti

Hugely popular, röstis pop up
everywhere nowadays. Try them
with other toppings, but they are
delicious served with creamed
horseradish and smoked fish.

Makes 30	**Ingredients**
Prep 20 minutes	500g (1lb 2oz) potatoes
Cook 12–18 minutes	1 tsp flour
Freezability No	½ tsp salt and ¼ tsp
	freshly ground
	black pepper
	2 tbsp sunflower oil
	Essential equipment
	large non-stick
	frying pan
	5cm (2in) round
	cookie cutter

GET AHEAD These can be made up to 2 days before
and stored in between layers of greaseproof paper in
an airtight container in the refrigerator.

COOK'S NOTE Make sure you squeeze out the potato
well before using, otherwise the röstis will fall apart.
When frying, fry lightly as they burn easily, but make
sure there is always some oil in the pan; this will help
them cook through evenly.

VARIATION You can add grated onion, finely chopped
spring onions or shallots, and fresh herbs to the rösti
mixture, but this adds more liquid, so add 1 egg to bind.

1 Using a potato or vegetable peeler, peel the
potatoes, then wash them in cold water and
dry them thoroughly in kitchen paper.

2 Using a box grater, coarsely grate the potatoes
onto a large plate. Don't use a food processor,
as they will become too wet. Use them immediately.

3 Place the potato in the centre of a clean tea towel.
Bring the corners of the towel together and squeeze
over the sink to remove as much moisture as possible.

4 Place the potato in a large mixing bowl, add the flour and seasoning, and mix well together with a wooden spoon.

5 Heat a frying pan with 1 tbsp sunflower oil. Place a cookie cutter in the pan and fill with 1 tsp of the potato mixture. Remove the ring.

6 Fry 1 rösti at first for about 2–3 minutes on each side, then taste to make sure you have the correct seasoning, adding more salt and pepper if required.

7 Using the cutter, shape and fry a further 9 röstis for 2–3 minutes on each side, pressing them down with the back of a teaspoon as they cook.

8 Once the röstis are crisp and golden, cool on kitchen paper. Repeat, using the remaining oil and mixture, to cook a further 10 röstis.

At this stage you can store the röstis, ready to use. Or top with your favourite ingredients, serve, and enjoy! Find this topping on p147.

Beetroot rösti with smoked trout and horseradish mousse

A seasonal canapé served with smoked salmon or smoked trout. It is best if you cook your own beetroot, but buy ready-cooked if short on time.

Makes 20

Ingredients

For the mousse
150g (5½oz) smoked trout
125g (4½oz) cream cheese
1 tbsp horseradish sauce
1 tbsp lemon juice
cayenne pepper

For the rösti
250g (9oz) cooked beetroot, grated
250g (9oz) potatoes, grated and squeezed dry
1 tbsp plain flour
1 egg, beaten
¾ tsp salt and ¼ tsp freshly ground black pepper
2 tbsp sunflower oil
paprika to garnish

Essential equipment
23cm (9in) non-stick frying pan
4.5cm (1¾in) fluted cookie cutter
piping bag with a large star nozzle

1 For the mousse, place the trout, cream cheese, horseradish, and lemon juice in a food processor or blender; pulse to a smooth paste. Add pepper to taste.

2 For the rösti, mix the beetroot, potato, flour, egg, and salt and pepper together. Heat 1 tbsp oil in the non-stick pan. Spread half the potato mixture, 0.5cm (¼in) thick, across the bottom of the pan. Reduce heat to low and cook until both sides are crisp and golden, about 10 minutes per side.

3 Remove from pan and cool slightly on kitchen paper. Heat the remaining oil. Cook and cool the remaining potato mixture.

4 Stamp out 10 rounds from each rösti with the cookie cutter. Cool completely before topping. Fill piping bag with mousse and pipe on to röstis. Sprinkle with paprika to garnish. Serve at room temperature.

....

GET AHEAD Make mousse up to 3 days in advance. Cover and refrigerate. Make rösti rounds up to 2 days in advance. Store in layers on greaseproof paper in an airtight container in the refrigerator. Crisp in preheated 200°C (400°F/Gas 6) oven for 5 minutes. Top and garnish up to 1 hour before serving.

Potato rösti with crème fraîche, caviar, and dill

These pan-fried potato cakes are perfect for serving at any special occasion. Make the röstis in advance and top just before serving.

Makes 20

Ingredients
500g (1lb 2oz) potatoes, grated and squeezed dry
1 tsp flour
¾ tsp salt and ¼ tsp freshly ground black pepper
2 tbsp sunflower oil
125ml (4fl oz) crème fraîche
100g (3½oz) black lumpfish caviar
20 dill sprigs to garnish

Essential equipment
23cm (9in) non-stick frying pan
4.5cm (1¾in) plain cookie cutter

1 Mix the potato, flour, and salt and pepper together. Heat 1 tbsp oil in the non-stick pan. Spread half the potato mixture, 0.5cm (¼in) thick, across the bottom of the pan. Reduce heat to low and cook until both sides are crisp and golden, about 10 minutes per side.

2 Remove from pan and cool slightly on kitchen paper. Heat the remaining oil. Cook and cool the remaining potato mixture.

3 Stamp out 10 rounds from each rösti with the cookie cutter. Cool completely before topping.

4 Top mini röstis with 1 tsp each crème fraîche and caviar. Garnish with dill sprigs. Serve warm.

GET AHEAD Make rösti rounds up to 2 days in advance. Store in layers on greaseproof paper in an airtight container in the refrigerator. Crisp in preheated 200°C (400°F/Gas 6) oven for 5 minutes. Top up to 45 minutes before serving.

Sweet potato and ginger rösti with coriander pesto

Full of flavour, these little cakes are an original slant on the classic rösti. Make in advance then assemble just in time to enjoy!

Makes 20

Ingredients

For the rösti
400g (14oz) orange sweet potato, peeled
3 spring onions, trimmed and finely chopped
1 egg
1 tbsp plain flour
1 tbsp grated fresh ginger
10g (¼oz) fresh coriander, finely chopped
salt and freshly ground black pepper
3 tbsp sunflower oil to fry

For the pesto
15g (½oz) fresh coriander
1 spring onion, trimmed
20g (¾oz) dry roast peanuts
1 tsp sesame oil
1–2 tbsp olive oil
1 green chilli, seeded

To garnish
120ml (4fl oz) crème fraîche

Essential equipment
large non-stick frying pan

1 Place the whole, peeled sweet potato in a small pan of cold salted water, bring to a boil, and boil for 5 minutes. Drain, cool, and coarsely grate the potato onto a plate. In a large bowl, mix together all the rösti ingredients except the oil.

2 Heat a large frying pan with a little oil. Shape 1 rösti into a small patty and fry in the oil for 1–2 minutes on each side just to check the seasoning. (This way you can see if more salt and pepper is needed.)

3 Now fry röstis in 2 batches, using a teaspoon and your fingers to help place the little mounds of sweet potato in the pan. Flatten as they cook. Make sure there is always a small amount of oil in the frying pan. Keep the heat medium-low so röstis do not burn. Allow to cool before topping.

4 For the pesto, place all the ingredients into a food processor or chop finely by hand to combine well. For the garnish, place 1 small tsp of crème fraîche and some pesto on top of each rösti.

....

GET AHEAD The rösti and pesto can be made the day before.

VARIATION Try topping with crème fraîche, a roll of smoked salmon, lime juice, and freshly ground black pepper.

Mini latkes with sour cream and apple sauce

Similar to the classic potato rösti with grated onion, these little latkes work well with either a fruit topping or smoked fish.

Makes 20

Ingredients

500g (1lb 2oz) potatoes, grated and squeezed dry
1 onion, grated and squeezed dry
1 tbsp plain flour
1 egg, beaten
¾ tsp salt and ¼ tsp freshly ground black pepper
2 tbsp sunflower oil
125ml (4fl oz) sour cream
125ml (4fl oz) apple sauce
2 tbsp finely chopped chives to garnish

1 Mix the potatoes, onion, flour, egg, and salt and pepper together.

2 Heat oil in a frying pan over medium heat. Working in batches, drop heaped teaspoonfuls of mixture into the hot oil. Use the back of the spoon to flatten them into thin pancakes. Cook, turning once, until crisp and golden on each side. Drain on kitchen paper. Cool slightly before topping.

3 Top latkes with 1 tsp each sour cream and apple sauce. Garnish with chopped chives. Serve warm or at room temperature.

GET AHEAD Make latkes up to 2 days in advance. Store in layers on greaseproof paper in an airtight container in the refrigerator. Crisp in preheated 200°C (400°F/Gas 6) oven for 5 minutes. Top up to 45 minutes before serving.

COOK'S NOTE The oaky, salty flavour of smoked fish perfectly complements these crispy potato pancakes. Try the classic combination of smoked salmon, sour cream, and a squeeze of lemon.

Crispy carrot and spring onion cakes with feta and black olive

Salty cheese and citrussy black olives are the perfect topping for these röstis. Squeeze the grated potato in a clean tea towel to remove excess moisture.

Makes 20

Ingredients
250g (9oz) carrots, grated
250g (9oz) potatoes, grated
and squeezed dry
2 spring onions, finely chopped
1 tbsp plain flour
1 egg, beaten
¾ tsp salt and ¼ tsp freshly
ground black pepper
2 tbsp sunflower oil
100g (3½oz) feta
cheese, crumbled
10 pitted black olives, quartered

1 Mix the carrot, potato, spring onion, flour, egg, and salt and pepper together.

2 Heat oil in a frying pan over medium heat. Working in batches, drop heaped teaspoonfuls of mixture into the hot oil. Use the back of the spoon to flatten them into thin pancakes. Cook, turning once, until crisp and golden on each side, 5 minutes per side. Drain on kitchen paper. Cool to room temperature before topping.

3 Divide feta cheese and olives among the cakes. Serve at room temperature.

....

GET AHEAD Make up to 2 days in advance. Store in layers on kitchen paper in an airtight container at room temperature. Crisp in a 200°C (400°F/Gas 6) oven for 3 minutes. Top 45 minutes before serving.

Spiced vegetable pakoras with tomato and ginger dipping sauce

These crisp and spicy pakoras are excellent served with raita, mango chutney, or this spicy tomato and ginger dipping sauce.

QUICK & EASY

Makes 15–20

Ingredients

For the sauce
150g (5½oz) tomato ketchup
½ tbsp grated fresh ginger
1 red chilli, seeded and finely chopped

For the cakes
60g (2oz) gram flour
½ tsp garam masala
½ tsp ground cumin
½ tsp ground turmeric
½ tsp chilli powder
½ tsp salt
15g (½oz) fresh coriander, chopped
1 aubergine
1 courgette
1 sweet potato, peeled
2 litres (3½ pints) vegetable or sunflower oil
sea salt

Essential equipment
deep-fat fryer or deep-sided saucepan

1 For the sauce, mix all the ingredients together and taste for seasoning. Set aside.

2 For the cakes, place all the ingredients for the batter into a large mixing bowl. Pour in 150ml (5fl oz) cold water, whisking until smooth. The batter should be thick and creamy.

3 Wash, dry, and slice the vegetables into thin discs about 5mm (¼in) thick. Dip the vegetables into the batter, coating well.

4 Heat the oil in a deep-fat fryer or deep-sided saucepan to 190°C (375°F/Gas 5), or until a cube of bread browns in 30 seconds. Drop the coated vegetables into the hot oil and fry until crisp, 3 minutes. Drain on kitchen paper and serve scattered with sea salt and tomato and ginger dipping sauce.

GET AHEAD The batter can be made 1 hour ahead. The sauce can be made a week ahead. The vegetables can be sliced hours ahead and kept covered and refrigerated.

VARIATION Other vegetables that are suitable for pakoras are sliced and peeled red onion, small florets of cauliflower, and thinly sliced fennel.

Gingered chicken cakes with coriander-lime mayonnaise

This version of an Asian-style fish cake is made with chicken. The cakes remain succulent after cooking and are best served warm.

Makes 20

Ingredients

For the cakes
2 boneless, skinless chicken breasts
2 tbsp fish sauce
2.5cm (1in) fresh ginger, roughly chopped
3 spring onions, roughly chopped
1 garlic clove, crushed
1 tsp salt
¼ tsp Tabasco sauce

For the dip
4 tbsp mayonnaise (see p88)
15g (½oz) coriander, finely chopped, plus 20 leaves to garnish
juice of 1 lime
2 tbsp diced mango to garnish

1 For the cakes, place all the cake ingredients in a food processor or blender; pulse until finely minced. Divide the mixture into 20 walnut-sized pieces. With wet hands, shape each piece into a ball and flatten into a cake.

2 Preheat a frying pan with a little oil and gently fry cakes for 1½ minutes on each side.

3 For the dip, combine the mayonnaise, chopped coriander, and lime.

4 Serve the cakes with the coriander-lime mayonnaise dip and scattered with mango and coriander leaves.

....

GET AHEAD Assemble the cakes and prepare the topping up to 1 day in advance. Cover and refrigerate. Keep at room temperature. Garnish and serve.

COOK'S NOTE Try using pork fillet instead of chicken and lemongrass instead of ginger for a tasty variation on these Asian-inspired minced cakes.

Crispy courgette goujons with parsley, lemon, and Parmesan

Everyone will adore these vegetarian goujons. Moist on the inside and crispy on the outside, serve with any flavoured mayonnaise.

QUICK & EASY

Makes 20

Ingredients
1 large courgette, trimmed
60g (2oz) fresh white bread
20g (¾oz) parsley
2 tbsp finely grated lemon zest
1 pinch cayenne pepper
30g (1oz) Parmesan cheese, grated, plus extra to serve
30g (1oz) plain flour
1 egg
1 litre (1¾ pints) vegetable oil
salt

Essential equipment
deep-sided saucepan

1 Slice the courgette in half and cut into about 20cm x 7.5cm (8in x 3in) long batons, do not remove the skin. Place the bread, parsley, lemon zest, pepper, and Parmesan into a food processor and blend until it resembles green crumbs.

2 Place the flour on a plate and whisk the egg in a shallow bowl. Place the breadcrumbs on a plate. Coat courgettes, a few at a time, in flour, then in egg, then roll well in herbed breadcrumbs until coated all over.

3 Preheat the oil in a deep-sided saucepan to 180°C (350°F/Gas 4), or until a cube of bread browns in 30 seconds. Fry the goujons in 4 batches of 5 goujons at a time until crisp, 1½–2 minutes.

4 Remove and scatter over salt and more grated Parmesan. Serve with aïoli (see p88).

....

GET AHEAD These can be made the day before, covered, and refrigerated to fry when needed. The breadcrumb mixture can be made several days ahead and kept in a dry cool place.

COOK'S NOTE Once fried you can keep these fritters warm in a medium hot oven for 30 minutes.

VARIATION You can use other herbs, cheeses, or chillies in the breadcrumb mixture.

Sesame prawn toasts

A classic Chinese starter, these delicious prawn toasts are an
all-time favourite. Serve simply with shoyu or soy sauce.

Makes 24

Ingredients
175g (6oz) raw prawns, peeled
3 spring onions
1 green chilli, seeded
1 tsp cornflour
1 garlic clove
1 tbsp grated fresh root ginger
15g (½oz) coriander
2 tbsp egg white
½ tsp salt
4 slices medium white bread
50g (1¾oz) sesame seeds
1 litre (1¾ pints) vegetable oil
for frying
Shoyu (Japanese soy sauce)
for dipping

Essential equipment
deep-sided saucepan

1 Place the prawns in a food processor with the spring
onions, chilli, cornflour, garlic, ginger, coriander, egg white,
and salt, and purée until smooth.

2 Divide prawn mixture among 4 slices of bread and spread
over evenly. Place sesame seeds on a plate and dip each slice
of bread prawn side down in the seeds to coat evenly.

3 Preheat the oil in a deep-sided saucepan to 180°C (350°F/Gas 4),
or until a cube of bread browns in 30 seconds. Fry toasts for
2 minutes on each side. Drain on kitchen paper.

4 Slice off crusts and accurately cut toast into 6 pieces.
Serve hot with a bowl of shoyu for dipping.

GET AHEAD You can make these the day ahead and keep covered
and chilled until ready to fry.

COOK'S NOTE If you are making this recipe in larger quantities,
you can keep them stacked on trays, with sheets of greaseproof
paper in between the layers and chill. If you are frying in a deep-fat
fryer it will have its own guideline as to how much oil it requires.

VARIATION If you do not like coriander, replace it with parsley.

Cocktail salmon and dill cakes with crème fraîche tartare

The secret ingredient here is the dash of Tabasco, which gives a kick to the delicate salmon flavour.

Makes 20

Ingredients

For the cakes
150g (5½oz) salmon fillet
200g (7oz) potatoes
2 tbsp roughly chopped dill
2 tbsp tomato ketchup
1 tsp horseradish sauce
1 tsp lemon juice
1 tsp salt
¼ tsp Tabasco
2 tbsp fresh breadcrumbs

For the topping
4 tbsp crème fraîche
1 tsp drained capers, finely chopped
1 tsp drained cocktail gherkins, finely chopped
1 tsp finely chopped tarragon
salt and freshly ground black pepper

To garnish
20 watercress sprigs

1 For the cakes, place the salmon in a pan of boiling water. Allow the water to return to a boil, then remove from the heat at once. Leave to cool completely. Drain on kitchen paper. Separate the cooked salmon into large flakes.

2 Preheat oven to 200°C (400°F/Gas 6). Cook the potatoes in boiling water until tender; mash until smooth. Combine potatoes with the salmon, dill, ketchup, horseradish sauce, and lemon. Add salt and Tabasco to taste.

3 Divide the mixture into 20 walnut-sized pieces, then shape into balls and roll in the breadcrumbs. Flatten into cakes and place on an oiled baking sheet. Bake until golden, 10 minutes. Cool to warm or room temperature.

4 For the topping, combine all the ingredients and add salt and pepper to taste. Spoon the topping on to the cakes. Garnish with watercress. Serve warm or at room temperature.

GET AHEAD Assemble the cakes and prepare the topping up to 1 day in advance. Cover and refrigerate. Bake and top the cakes up to 1 hour in advance. Keep at room temperature. Garnish just before serving.

Smoked haddock and parsley cakes

These smoked fish cakes combined with fresh herbs and mustard make perfect crowd pleasers, especially as winter warmers.

Makes 20

Ingredients
225g (8oz) smoked haddock fillet, skinned and boned
225g (8oz) mashed potatoes
salt and freshly ground black pepper
zest and juice of ½ lemon
20g (¾oz) flat-leaf parsley, finely chopped
1 tsp Dijon mustard
2 spring onions, finely chopped
2 eggs
60g (2oz) plain flour
60g (2oz) fresh or panko breadcrumbs
2 litres (3½ pints) vegetable or sunflower oil

To serve (optional)
sea salt
lemon wedges

Essential equipment
deep-fat fryer or deep-sided saucepan

1 Preheat oven to 180°C (350°F/Gas 4).

2 Place the smoked haddock in a buttered roasting tin, cover with foil, and bake for 15 minutes. Cool.

3 Flake the fish, checking for bones.

4 Place the fish in a large bowl and mix with the mashed potatoes, pepper to taste, lemon juice and zest, parsley, mustard, and spring onions. Taste to check the seasoning. You may need a little salt.

5 Whisk the eggs with 2 tbsp water. Put the flour and breadcrumbs in 2 separate shallow dishes. Roll fish mixture into walnut-sized balls; roll balls first in flour, then in egg, and then in breadcrumbs. Refrigerate until needed.

6 Preheat the oil in a deep-fat fryer or deep-sided saucepan to 190°C (375°F/Gas 5), or until a cube of bread browns in 30 seconds. Fry fish cakes in 4 batches of 5 fish cakes until golden and crisp, 2 minutes. Serve with sea salt and lemon wedges or a lemon or lime mayonnaise or tartar sauce (see p88).

....

GET AHEAD These freeze well. You can make these 2 days before serving.

COOK'S NOTE You can use smoked cod instead. Replace parsley with tarragon or chives.

Mini devilled crab cakes with tomato remoulade

These delicious mini crab cakes are sweet and light. Vary the herbs in the remoulade – try finely chopped basil or parsley, if you prefer.

Makes 20

Ingredients

For the cakes

250g (9oz) white crab meat
½ onion, finely chopped
½ tsp runny honey
½ tsp mustard powder
½ tsp Tabasco sauce
1 tsp Worcestershire sauce
1 tsp horseradish sauce
1 tsp lemon juice
3 tbsp mayonnaise (see p88)
2–4 tbsp fresh breadcrumbs, plus 45g (1½oz) fresh breadcrumbs for coating
salt and freshly ground black pepper
45g (1½oz) flour,
2 eggs, whisked
1 litre (1¾ pints) vegetable oil

For the remoulade

4 tbsp mayonnaise (see p88)
2 tsp finely chopped chives
1 tsp lemon juice
½ tsp creamy Dijon mustard
½ tsp finely chopped garlic
1 tomato, peeled, seeded, chopped, and diced
finely chopped chives to garnish

Essential equipment

deep-fat fryer or frying pan

1 For the cakes, mix the crab, onion, honey, mustard powder, Tabasco, Worcestershire, and horseradish sauces, lemon juice, and mayonnaise together. Add enough fresh breadcrumbs to bind, about 2–4 tbsp. Add salt and pepper to taste.

2 Divide the mixture into heaped teaspoonfuls, about 20 walnut-sized pieces. Shape each piece into a ball and roll in the flour, whisked eggs, and the remaining breadcrumbs. Refrigerate until firm, 30 minutes or overnight.

3 Preheat a deep-fat fryer or frying pan with oil to 180°C (350°F/ Gas 4), or until a cube of bread browns in 30 seconds. Fry cakes for 3 minutes until crisp and golden. Drain on kitchen paper.

4 For the remoulade, combine the mayonnaise, chives, lemon juice, mustard, and garlic. Add salt and pepper to taste. Garnish the cakes with tomato and chives and serve cakes warm or at room temperature with tomato remoulade.

GET AHEAD Assemble cakes and make remoulade up to 1 day in advance. Cover and refrigerate. Fry cakes up to 1 hour before serving and keep warm in a low oven.

VARIATION For Asian crab cakes, combine 250g (9oz) white crab meat; 3 spring onions, finely chopped; 1 red chilli, seeded and finely chopped; 2 tbsp mayonnaise (see p88); 1 tbsp finely grated fresh root ginger; grated zest of 1 lime; and salt and pepper. Taste for seasoning. Shape the mixture into 20 small balls and place on a baking sheet lined with greaseproof paper. Put 45g (1½oz) flour, 2 whisked eggs, and 60g (2oz) fresh breadcrumbs into 3 separate shallow dishes and roll the balls first in the flour, then in egg, and then in breadcrumbs. Chill for 30 minutes or overnight. Heat enough oil in a deep-sided saucepan to 180°C (350°F/Gas 4), or until a cube of bread browns in 30 seconds. Fry the cakes in batches of 5 until golden, 2–3 minutes. Drain on kitchen paper and serve with chilli-lime mayonnaise (see p88).

Aubergine and pine nut fritters with roast tomato sauce

A wonderful summery canapé, these little aubergine and cheese fritters are bursting with the flavours of the Mediterranean.

Makes 20

Ingredients

For the topping
2 plum tomatoes, halved
1 garlic clove, sliced
1 tsp balsamic vinegar
½ tsp runny honey
½ tsp finely chopped rosemary
salt and freshly ground
black pepper

For the fritters
2 tbsp olive oil
1 medium aubergine, diced
1 garlic clove, crushed
1 tbsp finely chopped parsley
1 tsp finely chopped rosemary
1 egg plus 1 egg yolk, beaten
75g (2½oz) Parmesan
cheese, grated
100g (3½oz) mozzarella
cheese, diced
60g (2oz) dry breadcrumbs
60g (2oz) pine nuts,
roughly chopped
salt and freshly ground
black pepper
20 small rocket leaves
to garnish

1 Preheat oven to 200°C (400°F/Gas 6).

2 For the topping, put the tomatoes and garlic on an oven tray. Drizzle with vinegar and honey and sprinkle with rosemary, and salt and pepper. Roast in oven until softened, 20 minutes. Cool and place in a food processor or blender; pulse until smooth.

3 For the fritters, heat the oil in a skillet over medium-high heat. Stir-fry the diced aubergine until soft and golden, 10 minutes. Drain and cool on kitchen paper.

4 Combine with the garlic, parsley, rosemary, beaten eggs, Parmesan, mozzarella, breadcrumbs, and pine nuts. Add salt and pepper to taste.

5 Divide the mixture into 20 walnut-sized pieces. Shape each piece into an oval. Place the ovals on an oiled baking sheet.

6 Bake until golden, 10 minutes. Cool to warm or room temperature. Spoon the topping on to the cakes. Garnish with rocket. Serve warm or at room temperature.

....

GET AHEAD Assemble the fritters and prepare topping up to 1 day in advance. Cover and refrigerate. Cook and top fritters up to 1 hour in advance. Keep at room temperature. Garnish just before serving.

VARIATION You could serve the topping as a dipping sauce for other canapés.

Dill pancakes with salmon caviar and lemon crème fraîche

Salmon, dill, and lemon are a winning combination in these delicate little pancakes. To save time, make the pancakes two days ahead.

QUICK & EASY

Makes 20

Ingredients

1 tsp grated lemon zest
1 tbsp lemon juice
125ml (4fl oz) crème fraîche
20 dill pancakes (see below)
100g (3½oz) salmon caviar
20 dill sprigs to garnish

1 Mix the lemon zest and juice into crème fraîche.

2 Top each pancake with 1 tsp each crème fraîche and salmon caviar. Garnish with dill. Serve at room temperature.

GET AHEAD Make lemon crème fraîche up to 1 day in advance. Cover and refrigerate. Top pancakes up to 45 minutes before serving.

VARIATION Top with smoked salmon instead of salmon caviar if you prefer.

HERB PANCAKES

Makes 20 | 60g (2oz) plain flour; ¼ tsp baking powder; ¼ tsp salt; 1 egg, beaten; 3 tbsp milk; 1 tbsp finely chopped fresh herbs; 1 tbsp sunflower oil

Sift the flour, baking powder, and salt together. Make a well in the centre. Add the egg and milk to the well. Gradually draw in flour and mix to a smooth batter. Stir in the herbs. Brush a frying pan or griddle with oil. Preheat over medium heat. Working in batches, drop heaped teaspoonfuls of mixture into the hot pan. Cook until bubbles appear and underside is golden, 3 minutes. Turn and brown other side, 2 minutes. Brush pan with more oil between each batch of pancakes. Cool pancakes. Serve at room temperature.

GET AHEAD Make pancakes up to 2 days in advance. Store in an airtight container in the refrigerator. Crisp in preheated 200°C (400°F/Gas 6) oven for 3 minutes.

VARIATIONS
Dill pancakes Add 1 tbsp finely chopped dill to the ingredients.
Chive pancakes Add 1 tbsp finely chopped chives to the ingredients.

Chive pancakes with crème fraîche and red onion confit

An all-time favourite, these mini pancakes can be made up to two days in advance and topped just before the party.

QUICK & EASY

Makes 20

Ingredients
2 tbsp caster sugar
1 tbsp water
1 tbsp red wine vinegar
1 medium red onion, finely sliced
salt and freshly ground black pepper
20 chive pancakes (see opposite)
125ml (4fl oz) crème fraîche
1 tbsp finely chopped fresh chives

1 Put the sugar and water in a small pan and stir to dissolve. Bring to a boil over medium-low heat and cook to a dark caramel. Remove from heat and add vinegar and onions.

2 Return to a medium heat and stir-fry until onions soften, 5 minutes. Add salt and pepper to taste. Cool to warm.

3 Top each pancake with 1 tsp each crème fraîche and onions. Garnish with chives. Serve at room temperature.

....

GET AHEAD Make onion confit up to 1 day in advance. Cover and store at room temperature. Top pancakes up to 45 minutes before serving.

tartlets and parcels

Step-by-step Filo tartlets

These mini tartlet bases are suited to so many different fillings, so have fun inventing your own. Make in advance and fill on the day of the party.

Makes 20–25
Prep 20 minutes
Cook 6–8 minutes
Freezability No

Ingredients
4 sheets of filo pastry
(20cm x 25cm/
8in x 10in)
2 tbsp melted butter

Essential equipment
24-hole mini muffin tin

GET AHEAD Make the tartlets up to 1 month in advance and store in an airtight container at room temperature.

COOK'S NOTE To prevent the filo pastry from drying out or cracking during use, keep it covered with a slightly damp cloth. You may find it easier to have a little bowl of flour at hand while assembling, to dip your fingers in, so your fingers do not stick to the pastry.

VARIATION Sprinkle finely grated Parmesan in between each layer of filo pastry.

1 Preheat oven to 180°C (350°F/Gas 4). Lay the filo pastry down on a cool surface or large chopping board. Cover any unused pastry with a clean tea towel.

2 Working with one pastry sheet at a time, brush the pastry evenly with a little of the melted butter, making sure the rest of the pastry is covered.

3 Using a sharp knife, carefully cut the buttered pastry sheet into even-sized squares, 5cm x 5cm (2in x 2in).

4 Carefully pick up one square at a time and place on top of each other using 4 squares at different angles to create a spiky look.

7 Remove the tartlets from the mini muffin tin and cool completely, then store the filo tartlets in an airtight container until ready to use.

5 Push the pastry stack into the mini muffin tin ensuring the bottom of the filo tartlet is as flat as possible otherwise the filling will fall out.

6 Repeat until all the filo pastry has been used up then bake in the oven for about 6–8 minutes until golden brown and crisp. Allow to cool slightly.

Arrange the filo tartlets on a large serving tray, fill with your chosen filling, and watch them disappear in minutes! Find this filling on p170.

Filo tartlets with spicy coriander prawns

These tartlets are a great party stand-by, perfect for when friends suddenly pop in for a drink, as they take just minutes to prepare.

QUICK & EASY

Makes 20

Ingredients
2 tsp sesame seeds
125g (4½oz) medium prawns, cooked and peeled
15g (½oz) coriander, chopped
6 tbsp Thai sweet chilli sauce
20 filo tartlets (see pp166–7)

1 Toast the seeds in a dry pan over low heat until golden brown, 3 minutes. Combine the prawns, coriander, and chilli sauce.

2 Spoon into tartlets and garnish with the toasted seeds.

....

GET AHEAD Make filling up to 1 day in advance. Cover and refrigerate. Fill tartlets up to 45 minutes before serving.

COOK'S NOTE If using frozen cooked prawns, defrost in a colander. When defrosted, squeeze out water with your hands and pat dry with kitchen paper.

Filo tartlets with smoked chicken, black olives, and parsley pesto

Smoked chicken breast, black olives, and pine nuts are a perfect filling for these mini filo tartlets. They are best served at room temperature.

QUICK & EASY

Makes 20

Ingredients
15g (½oz) parsley
1 garlic clove, crushed
4 tbsp pine nuts
4 tbsp Parmesan cheese, grated
juice of ½ lemon
2 tbsp olive oil
salt and freshly ground black pepper
1 smoked chicken breast
20 filo tartlets (see pp166–7)
10 stoned black olives, halved

1 For the pesto, place the parsley, garlic, pine nuts, Parmesan, lemon juice, and oil in a food processor or blender; pulse to a thick paste. Add salt and pepper to taste.

2 Cut the chicken into thin strips, 0.5cm (¼in) wide.

3 Put 1 tsp pesto into each tartlet. Arrange chicken strips on top. Garnish with half an olive. Serve at room temperature.

GET AHEAD Make pesto up to 3 days in advance. Cover and refrigerate. Fill tartlets up to 45 minutes before serving.

Filo tartlets with Asian beef salad

Melting mouthfuls of beef are tossed in a delicious combination of Asian flavours. Seed the chilli for the garnish, if you prefer.

Makes 20

Ingredients

200g (7oz) beef fillet steak, 2.5cm (1in) thick
1 tbsp light soy sauce
1 tbsp lime juice
1 tbsp fish sauce
¼ tsp sugar
15g (½oz) coriander, leaves stripped
15g (½oz) mint, leaves stripped, plus extra to garnish
¼ red pepper, finely diced
1 tomato, seeded and diced
1 tsp sesame seeds
1 tsp grated lime zest
20 filo tartlets (see pp166–7)
1 sliced red chilli to garnish

1 Sear the steak in a hot pan on both sides, 6 minutes in total. Cool and cut into 20 slices.

2 Toss the steak slices with the soy, lime juice, fish sauce, sugar, fresh herbs, pepper, tomato, sesame seeds, and lime zest. Divide steak slices among the filo tartlets. Garnish with red chilli and mint leaves.

GET AHEAD Make the filling up to 1 day in advance, but only add the fresh herbs up to 1 hour before serving. Cover and refrigerate. Fill the tartlets up to 30 minutes before serving.

Step-by-step
Shortcrust pastry tartlets

These pastry tartlets can be used for many different occasions – at Christmas fill with mincemeat and cream, or in the summer with roasted vegetables and pesto.

Makes 25–30
Prep 15 minutes, plus 30 minutes chilling
Cook 15 minutes
Freezability Yes

Ingredients
175g (6oz) plain flour, sifted
¼ tsp salt
85g (3oz) chilled butter, diced
1 egg

Essential equipment
5cm (2in) round cookie cutter
2 x 24-hole mini muffin tins

GET AHEAD Make the pastry up to 2 days ahead and refrigerate. Bring back to room temperature before rolling out. The tartlets can be made a week ahead, but may need to be refreshed in a hot oven for several minutes to crisp.

COOK'S NOTE The best way to blind bake pastry tartlets is shown here, but to save time, prick the base with a fork and freeze, then bake from frozen until crisp, 15 minutes.

VARIATION For sweet pastry, add 1 tbsp icing sugar, soft brown sugar, or caster sugar. Add 1 tbsp ground almonds, hazelnuts, walnuts, and orange zest. For savoury pastry, add chopped herbs, spices, grated Parmesan, or olives.

1 Place the flour, salt, and diced butter into a large mixing bowl. Alternatively, you can use a food processor. Preheat oven to 200°C (400°F/Gas 6).

2 Using your fingertips, rub the butter into the flour until the mixture resembles breadcrumbs. Alternatively, pulse in the food processor.

3 Add 1 egg and, using your fingertips or a table knife, mix well, adding enough water as necessary, about 1–2 tbsp to bring the dough together.

4 Using your hands, bring the dough together completely and turn out onto a lightly floured cool surface. Knead the pastry gently into a smooth round.

5 Using a rolling pin, roll out the pastry on a lightly floured surface to form a large circle, about 3mm (⅛in) thick.

6 Using a cookie cutter, stamp out 25–30 rounds. Roll out the pastry for a second time using the excess pastry to cut out the remaining or extra rounds.

7 Carefully push the pastry into the base of a mini muffin tin and prick the base several times with a fork. Refrigerate for 30 minutes or freeze.

8 Line each tartlet with greaseproof paper and fill with baking beans. Bake for 10 minutes. Remove paper and beans and bake for 5–10 minutes. Cool.

Once cool, place the pastry tartlets on a flat serving tray and fill with various fillings. Choose from the delicious fillings on pp174–7.

Oriental chicken with spicy pesto tartlets

This flavourful filling also works well in a filo tartlet. The chicken and pesto can be prepared in advance, but fill the tartlets on the day of the party.

Makes 20

Ingredients
1 boneless, skinless
chicken breast
2 tbsp light soy sauce
1 tbsp rice vinegar
1 tbsp sesame oil
1 tbsp sunflower oil

For the pesto
15g (½oz) coriander
10 mint leaves
1 green chilli, seeded
1 spring onion
1 tbsp roasted peanuts
1 tbsp sesame oil
25–30 pastry tartlets
(see pp172–3)

1 Place the chicken in a pan and cover it with cold water. Bring to a simmer over low heat. Simmer gently without boiling until cooked through, 7–10 minutes. Cool completely in cooking liquid.

2 Drain and shred chicken. Toss chicken with the soy, vinegar, sesame and sunflower oils.

3 For the pesto, place the coriander, mint, chilli, spring onion, peanuts, and oil in a food processor or blender; pulse to a thick paste.

4 Fill tartlets with chicken and top with pesto. Serve at room temperature.

....

GET AHEAD Cook chicken up to 2 days in advance. Cover and refrigerate. Prepare pesto up to 2 days in advance. Cover and refrigerate. Fill tartlets up to 1 hour before serving.

Mushroom and chive hollandaise tartlets

These tartlets are full of woody forest flavours and, topped with a contrasting creamy sharp hollandaise, are perfect to serve on any occasion.

Makes 20

Ingredients
30g (1oz) butter
1 shallot, finely chopped
200g (7oz) field
mushrooms, chopped
1 tbsp cream cheese
2 tbsp lemon juice
salt and freshly ground
black pepper
25–30 pastry tartlets
(see pp172–3)
175ml (6fl oz) hollandaise
(see p89)
1 bunch of chives,
finely chopped

1 Preheat oven to 200°C (400°F/Gas 6).

2 Heat the butter in a skillet. Add the shallots and mushrooms. Stir-fry over high heat until softened, 5 minutes. Cool slightly.

3 Place mushroom mixture, cream cheese, and lemon juice in a food processor or blender; pulse to a rough purée. Add salt and pepper to taste.

4 Divide mushroom mixture among tartlets. Put 1 tsp hollandaise on top and heat through in the oven for 5 minutes. Sprinkle with chives. Serve warm.

GET AHEAD Make mushroom mixture up to 3 days in advance. Cover and refrigerate. Fill tartlets up to 1 hour before serving. Store at room temperature.

COOK'S NOTE If you are short of time, use ready-made hollandaise.

Feta, olive, and rosemary tartlets

Use the best-quality ingredients to make these mini mouthfuls, reminiscent of Greek cuisine. The tartlets are best served warm.

Makes 20

Ingredients

60g (2oz) feta cheese, crumbled
20 baked pastry tartlets
(see pp172–3)
1 egg yolk
3 tbsp double cream
freshly ground black pepper
10 pitted black olives, halved
20 rosemary sprigs to garnish

1 Preheat oven to 180°C (350°F/Gas 4).

2 Divide the feta among the tartlets. Beat the egg and cream together. Add pepper to taste. Spoon the egg mixture into tartlets.

3 Top with the olive halves and rosemary sprigs. Bake until golden and set, 7 minutes. Serve warm.

....

GET AHEAD Bake up to 2 days in advance. Store in an airtight container in the refrigerator. Warm through in a preheated 150°C (300°F/Gas 2) oven for 10 minutes.

Herbed prawn wonton crescents with a tangy lime dipping sauce

Impress your guests with these tasty little prawn wontons full of the flavours of the Far East. You can also use ready-made wrappers.

Makes 20

Ingredients
75g (2½oz) prawns, cooked and peeled
2 spring onions, chopped
2 tbsp chopped coriander
1cm (½in) piece ginger, grated
1 tbsp fish sauce
20 wonton wrappers (see below) or 20 ready-made dumpling wrappers

For the sauce
juice of 1 lime
1 tbsp sugar
2 tbsp fish sauce

Essential equipment
wok with a lid

1 Place the prawns, spring onions, coriander, ginger, and fish sauce in food processor or blender; pulse until finely chopped.

2 Place ½ tsp prawn filling in the centre of each wrapper. Fold wrapper over to enclose filling to make crescents. Press edges together to seal. With fingertips, crimp edges. Dip the bottom of each wonton crescent in a little flour. Place on a floured oven tray and cover with a damp tea towel.

3 For the sauce, combine the lime juice with sugar and fish sauce. Heat 1 tbsp oil in the wok over medium heat. When oil is very hot, add half the wonton crescents flat-side down to the wok in a single layer. Cook until crispy underneath, 5 minutes.

4 Add to the centre of the wok enough water to come about halfway up the sides of each wonton crescent. Cover wok with the lid and cook until all the liquid has evaporated, 10 minutes.

5 Remove wontons from the wok, cover with foil, and keep warm in a preheated 120°C (250°F/Gas ½) oven. Repeat with remaining oil, wonton crescents, and water. Serve warm with tangy lime dipping sauce.

WONTON WRAPPERS
Makes 20 | 150g (5½oz) plain flour; 125ml (4fl oz) boiling water | Essential equipment: 5cm (2in) plain cookie cutter

Place the flour in a bowl and make a well in the centre. Pour in the water. Mix with a fork to form a rough dough. Cover with a tea towel and let stand until cool enough to handle. Knead on a lightly floured surface until smooth and elastic, 5 minutes. Cover with a tea towel and let rest for 30 minutes. Roll out dough on a lightly floured surface to a 0.25cm (⅛in) thickness. Stamp out 20 rounds with the cookie cutter.

GET AHEAD Make up to 1 day in advance. Store in an airtight container stacked in single layers separated by greaseproof paper. Alternatively, freeze wrappers up to 1 month in advance. Store in a sealed plastic freezer bag stacked in single layers separated by cling film. Defrost overnight in the refrigerator.

Wonton crescents with gingered pork and chilli soy dipping sauce

These wontons are delicious and well worth the effort. Prepare the filling and dipping sauce in advance.

Makes 20

Ingredients

75g (2½oz) lean minced pork
1 garlic clove, crushed
1 spring onion, chopped
2cm (¾in) piece ginger, grated
1 tbsp dark soy sauce
1 tsp sesame oil
20 wonton wrappers (see opposite) or 20 ready-made round dumpling wrappers
2 tbsp sunflower oil
250ml (9fl oz) cold water for cooking

For the sauce

1 tbsp Chinese hot chilli sauce
4 tbsp dark soy sauce

Essential equipment

wok with a lid

1 Place the pork, garlic, spring onion, ginger, soy, and sesame oil in a food processor or blender; pulse until well combined.

2 Place ½ tsp pork filling in the centre of each wrapper. Fold wrapper over to enclose filling to make crescents. Press edges together to seal. With fingertips, crimp edges. Dip the bottom of each wonton crescent in a little flour. Place on a floured oven tray and cover with a damp tea towel.

3 For the sauce, combine the chilli sauce and soy.

4 Heat 1 tbsp oil in the wok over medium heat. When oil is very hot, add half of the wonton crescents flat-side down to the wok in a single layer. Cook until crispy underneath, 5 minutes.

5 Add to the centre of the wok enough water to come about halfway up the sides of each wonton crescent. Cover wok with the lid and cook until all the liquid has evaporated, 10 minutes.

6 Remove wontons from the wok, cover with foil, and keep warm in a preheated oven 120°C (250°F/Gas ½). Repeat with remaining oil, wonton crescents, and water. Serve warm with chilli soy dipping sauce.

....

GET AHEAD Assemble wonton crescents up to 3 hours in advance. Store covered with cling film on a floured oven tray in the refrigerator. Alternatively, freeze up to 1 month in advance. Defrost overnight in the refrigerator. Fry up to 45 minutes before serving. Keep warm, covered in a preheated 120°C (250°F/Gas ½) oven.

COOK'S NOTE It's the flour that makes the wonton crescents crispy. If assembling ahead of time, dip the wonton crescents again in flour before cooking for maximum crispiness.

Spiced squash samosas with yogurt-harissa dip

These samosas can be made two days ahead or even frozen. Any type of squash works, so experiment with your favourite flavours.

Makes 25

Ingredients

For the samosas
2 tbsp olive oil
1 small white onion, finely chopped
1 garlic clove, finely chopped
½ tsp fennel seeds
pinch of chilli powder
½ tbsp grated fresh root ginger
225g (8oz) butternut squash, peeled, seeded, and cut into small cubes
salt and freshly ground black pepper
100g (3½oz) cream cheese
50g (1¾oz) frozen peas
2 tbsp chopped fresh mint leaves
1 egg white
5 sheets filo pastry (25cm x 46cm/10in x 18in)
melted butter or beaten egg to glaze

For the dip
150g (5½oz) Greek-style yogurt
1 tsp harissa paste
1 tbsp chopped fresh mint leaves

1 Heat the oil in a large frying pan and sauté the onion and garlic until soft but not coloured. Add the fennel seeds, chilli, ginger, and diced squash and cook gently until squash is cooked through. Season with salt and pepper.

2 Add the cream cheese, peas, and mint and cook through for a few minutes. Stir until well combined. Taste to check the seasoning and cool.

3 For the dip, combine all the ingredients and taste; it may need more harissa paste.

4 To assemble the samosas, preheat oven to 180°C (350°F/Gas 4).

5 Whisk the egg white with 1 tbsp cold water. Place a sheet of filo pastry onto a cool surface and lightly brush with egg white. Cut the filo into strips (5cm/2in).

6 Place a small teaspoon of the squash mixture at top right corner. Carefully fold the left-hand corner over the right in a perfect triangle, continue to fold down until you reach the bottom of the strip of pastry.

7 Place on a baking tray lined with greaseproof paper and glaze with the melted butter or beaten egg. Bake until lightly golden and crisp, 10–12 minutes. Serve with yogurt and harissa dip.

....

GET AHEAD These can be made 2 days ahead and also freeze well.

Spicy pork empanaditas with chunky avocado relish

These tasty little parcels of spicy pork are served with a robust relish. The raisins in the filling complement the meat and spices perfectly.

Makes 20

Ingredients

For the filling
1 tbsp sunflower oil
½ medium onion, finely chopped
175g (6oz) minced pork
3 garlic cloves, finely chopped
1 red chilli, seeded and finely chopped
½ tsp ground cumin
¼ tsp ground cinnamon
pinch of ground cloves
125ml (4fl oz) tomato juice
1 tsp tomato purée
2 tbsp raisins
10 pimento-stuffed green olives, chopped
salt and freshly ground black pepper

For the pastry
175g (6oz) flour
½ tsp salt
30g (1oz) butter
90ml (3fl oz) warm water

1 For the filling, heat the oil in a frying pan over medium heat. Stir-fry onions in oil until soft, 5 minutes.

2 Add the pork. Stir pork constantly with a fork to break up any lumps, until lightly browned, 5 minutes. Add garlic and chilli and cook until fragrant, 3 minutes. Add spices, tomato juice, tomato purée, raisins, and olives.

3 Reduce heat to low and simmer, stirring occasionally, until thick, 15 minutes. Cool. Add salt and pepper to taste. Cover and refrigerate until chilled, 30 minutes.

4 For the pastry, sift the flour and salt into a bowl. Rub the butter into the flour with fingers until the mixture resembles fine crumbs. Use a fork to stir in the water to make a firm dough.

5 Turn dough on to a lightly floured surface and knead until smooth, 3 minutes. Wrap dough in cling film and let rest at room temperature for 30 minutes.

6 Roll out dough to a 2mm (⅛in) thickness. Stamp out 20 rounds with the cookie cutter. Place 1 tsp of filling in the centre of each round.

7 Fold pastry over filling to make crescents. Pinch edges firmly together to seal. With fingertips, crimp edges. Place empanaditas on oiled baking sheets. Brush with beaten egg. Bake until crisp and golden, 15 minutes. Cool on a wire rack.

For the relish
½ medium onion,
finely chopped
2 red chillies, seeded
and finely chopped
2 tomatoes, peeled, seeded,
and finely chopped
1 garlic clove, finely chopped
2 tbsp finely chopped coriander
juice of 1 lime
2 medium avocados
salt

Essential equipment
1 plain cookie cutter
(6.5cm/2¾in)

8 For the relish, combine the onion, chilli, tomato, garlic, coriander, and lime juice. Cut the avocados into cubes (2.5cm/1in). Mash the avocado into the onion mixture while combining with the other ingredients. Add salt to taste.

9 Cover cling film tightly over the surface of the relish. Refrigerate for 15 minutes. Serve empanaditas warm or at room temperature with relish for dipping.

....

GET AHEAD Assemble empanaditas up to 1 day in advance. Cover and refrigerate. Bake empanaditas up to 8 hours in advance. Keep at room temperature. Make relish up to 3 hours in advance. Cover tightly with cling film and refrigerate.

COOK'S NOTE The secret to juicy empanaditas is to chill the filling before assembling. The juices in the filling will solidify so that the empanaditas won't leak as they are assembled. Press a piece of cling film directly on to the surface of the relish to keep out the air that causes the avocado to darken. If the relish does discolour slightly, simply scrape off the dark surface. The relish will still be green underneath.

VARIATION
Spicy chorizo empanaditas Use 175g (6oz) skinned and crumbled chorizo sausage instead of minced pork when making the filling.

Hot pepper and smoky mozzarella empanaditas Make hot pepper relish (see p132). Fill the pastry rounds with 1 tsp grated smoked mozzarella and 1 tsp relish instead of spicy pork mixture.

wraps, rolls, and finger sandwiches

Rolled ricotta and sage crêpes with Parmesan shavings

These crêpes can be filled and rolled the day before and then just sliced to serve. They are best served chilled or at room temperature.

Makes 20

Ingredients

200g (7oz) ricotta cheese
1 tbsp finely chopped sage
1 tbsp finely chopped parsley
1 tbsp grated Parmesan cheese
nutmeg
salt and freshly ground
black pepper
5 sage crêpes (see below)
20 Parmesan shavings to garnish

1 For the filling, combine the ricotta, herbs, and Parmesan until well combined. Add the nutmeg and salt and pepper to taste.

2 Spread ricotta mixture evenly over the crêpes. Roll up tightly. Wrap in cling film. Twist the ends to secure. Refrigerate rolls for 1 hour. Trim untidy ends with a serrated knife.

3 Cut each rolled crêpe into 4 slices. Discard the cling film after slicing. Garnish with Parmesan shavings. Serve chilled or at room temperature.

GET AHEAD Roll crêpes up to 1 day in advance. Cover and refrigerate. Cut and garnish up to 1 hour before serving.

CRÊPES

Makes 5 | 60g (2oz) plain flour; ¼ tsp salt; 1 egg, beaten; 150ml (5fl oz) milk; 30g (1oz) butter | **Essential equipment: 23cm (9in) non-stick frying pan**

Sift the flour and salt into a bowl. Make a well in the centre and add the egg. Gradually beat in flour from the sides. Whisking constantly, slowly pour in the milk to make a smooth batter. Cover and let stand at room temperature for 30 minutes. Melt butter in the pan over medium heat. Swirl butter to coat base of pan. Pour excess melted butter into a bowl and reserve. Pour a small ladle of batter into the pan. Tilt the pan and swirl the batter to cover the entire base of the pan. Cook until golden underneath, 1 minute. Flip crêpe over with a rubber spatula and cook until golden underneath, 30 seconds more. Remove from pan. Repeat with reserved butter and remaining batter. Discard any thick or torn crêpes. Cool crêpes completely.

GET AHEAD Make crêpes up to 2 days in advance. Store in an airtight container stacked in single layers separated by greaseproof paper. Alternatively, freeze crêpes up to 1 month in advance. Store in a sealed plastic freezer bag stacked in single layers separated by plastic wrap. Defrost overnight in refrigerator.

COOK'S NOTE Be sure to add the milk gradually while whisking constantly in order to achieve a perfectly smooth batter. If lumps do occur, pour the batter through a sieve. Alternatively, make batter in a food processor or blender; pulse flour, salt, eggs, and milk until smooth.

VARIATION For sage crêpes, add 1 tbsp finely chopped sage to the ingredients.

Chive-tied crêpe bundles with smoked salmon and lemon crème fraîche

Attractive and classic, these delicious crêpe bundles are perfect for the festive season or any other elegant occasion.

Makes 20

Ingredients
20 long chives
5 crêpes (see opposite)
grated zest of 1 lemon
125ml (4fl oz) crème fraîche
250g (9oz) smoked salmon slices, chopped
2 tbsp finely chopped chives
freshly ground black pepper

Essential equipment
8.5cm (3¼in) plain cookie cutter

1 Drop the long chives into a pan of boiling water. Drain and rinse immediately under cold water. Pat dry on kitchen paper.

2 Stamp out 4 rounds from each crêpe with the cookie cutter. Combine the lemon zest, crème fraîche, and smoked salmon. Place 1 tsp of the mixture in the centre of each crêpe.

3 Sprinkle with chives and a pinch of pepper. Carefully bring the edges of each crêpe together into a little bundle. Tie each bundle with a long chive. Refrigerate until chilled, 15 minutes.

....

GET AHEAD Make crêpe bundles up to 4 hours in advance. Store in single layers covered with cling film in the refrigerator.

COOK'S NOTE To make classic beggars' purses, omit chopped chives and pepper and replace crème fraîche with sour cream and salmon with black caviar.

6 ways with **wraps**

Tortilla wraps are a wonderful base for colourful and tasty salads, but make sure the flavours are strong and the filling is not too dry. These recipes make 18–20 wraps.

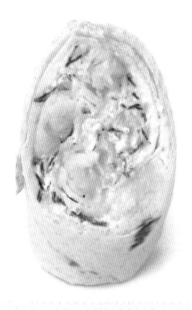

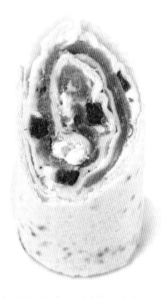

citrus prawn wraps

Mix together 200g (7oz) small prawns with 175g (6oz) cream cheese or soft goat's cheese, salt and black pepper, grated zest of 1 lemon, and a small handful of chopped herbs such as chervil, dill, chives, and basil. Heat a large dry frying pan and warm through 3 large tortillas quickly, one at a time, on both sides. Spread the prawn mixture over the surface and roll up as tightly as possible. Wrap in cling film and refrigerate until needed. Slice each wrap into 6–7 pieces on a sharp angle to serve.

chicken Caesar salad wrap

Shred 150g (5½oz) cooked chicken breast and mix with 3 tbsp Caesar mayonnaise (see p121). Heat a large dry frying pan and warm through 3 tortillas quickly, one at a time, on both sides. Spread the chicken (make sure it is moist, adding more mayonnaise if necessary) over each wrap, scatter over ½ finely shredded cos lettuce and 75g (2½oz) Parmesan shavings, and roll up as tightly as possible. Wrap in cling film and refrigerate until needed. Slice each wrap into 6–7 wedges on a sharp angle to serve.

smoked trout and red pepper cream wraps

Preheat grill. Grill 2 seeded and quartered red peppers, skin side up, for 7 minutes, or until blackened. Place in a plastic bag to cool, remove the charred skin, and slice into strips. Combine 150g (5½oz) goat's cheese or cream cheese, grated zest of 1 lemon, black pepper, 15g (½oz) chopped chervil, and 1 tsp creamed horseradish. Warm through 3 tortillas, one at a time. Spread with the cream and scatter with the pepper and 115g (4oz) smoked salmon. Roll up, wrap, and chill. Cut on an angle to serve.

Know-how... preparing wraps

GET AHEAD Slice up to 1 hour before serving but keep well covered.

COOK'S NOTE Warming the tortilla briefly before filling and rolling makes it far more pliable. To warm the tortillas, heat a large dry frying pan and heat the tortillas through quickly, one at a time on both sides. Do not overfill the wrap and ensure the ingredients are equally distributed. Make sure the filled tortillas are rolled up tightly in cling film and chilled, then use a sharp non-serrated knife to cut them diagonally into 6 portions.

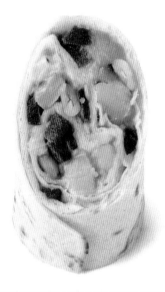

grilled spiced pepper and chorizo wrap

Preheat grill. Seed and quarter 1 each large red and yellow pepper and grill, skin side up, until charred. Cool in a plastic bag, remove the skin, slice thinly, and mix with 2 tbsp chopped basil and coriander, salt and black pepper, ¼ tsp balsamic vinegar, 1 tsp olive oil, and ¼ tsp dried chilli flakes. Warm through 3 tortillas. Spread 125g (4½oz) cream cheese over the wraps and scatter with the pepper mix and 15 slices of chorizo (5 slices each). Roll up tightly, wrap, and refrigerate until needed. Slice on an angle to serve.

hoisin–chilli duck wraps

Preheat oven to 180°C (350°F/Gas 4). Rub 1 tbsp soy sauce, 1 tsp honey, and ¼ tsp Chinese five spice powder into 2 duck legs. Cover tightly with foil (no gaps) and roast for 1 hour, or until starting to fall apart. Remove the meat off the legs and shred, then mix in 2 tbsp hoisin sauce. Warm 3 tortillas. Spread meat over each wrap and scatter with 1 thumb julienned fresh ginger, 1 seeded and julienned red chilli, ½ cucumber, julienned, and 10g (¼oz) chopped coriander. Roll up. Slice off the last 5cm (2in) and wrap for 1 hour before slicing.

avocado, basil, and pine nut wraps

Toast 30g (1oz) pine nuts in a dry frying pan for several minutes. Mix together with 1 ripe diced avocado, 2 tbsp mayonnaise (see p88), salt and black pepper, pinch of cayenne, 1 tbsp lemon juice, 2 tbsp finely grated Parmesan, and 2 finely chopped spring onions. Warm through 3 tortillas. Spread over the avocado mixture, scatter with basil leaves and ½ seeded and thinly sliced red pepper, and roll up tightly in cling film. Cover and refrigerate until needed. Slice on an angle to serve.

Crab and papaya rice paper rolls with sweet chilli dipping sauce

These rolls are so fresh, and with clean and vibrant flavours they will be popular with everyone. You can buy rice paper from large supermarkets.

QUICK & EASY

Makes 20

Ingredients
125g (4½oz) white crab meat
2 spring onions, cut into julienne strips
½ cucumber, seeded and cut into julienne strips
10 sheets of rice paper
1 papaya, quartered and finely sliced
20 mint leaves
20 basil leaves

For the sauce
2 tbsp sugar
2 tbsp boiling water
2 tbsp fish sauce
2 tbsp lime juice
1 tbsp rice vinegar
1 red chilli, seeded and chopped
1 garlic, crushed

1 Divide the crab, spring onions, and cucumber strips into 20 equal-sized portions.

2 Pour about 1.5cm (¾in) cold water into a shallow dish. Dip 1 sheet of rice paper into the water and leave to soften, 2 minutes. Remove and spread out on a dry tea towel. Cut in half.

3 Top 1 half with 1 portion of crab, spring onion, and cucumber. Place 1 papaya slice, 1 mint leaf, and 1 basil leaf on top of the cucumber so that they stick out slightly over the straight end of the rice paper. Roll rice paper over to enclose the filling.

4 Fold one end of the rice paper over the enclosed filling to make a 5cm (2in) cylinder. Continue rolling up into a cylinder and press the end with a wet finger to seal.

5 Place the roll, seal side down, on a tray and cover with a dampened tea towel to keep moist. Repeat with the remaining half sheet of rice paper, then start again with remaining rice paper sheets and filling.

6 For the sauce, dissolve the sugar in boiling water. Combine dissolved sugar, fish sauce, lime juice, vinegar, chilli, and garlic.

7 Serve rice paper rolls chilled or at room temperature with sweet chilli dipping sauce.

....

GET AHEAD Prepare filling ingredients up to 1 day in advance. Cover and refrigerate. Make rolls up to 3 hours in advance. Cover with a dampened tea towel and refrigerate. Be sure to keep the tea towel moist.

COOK'S NOTE Rice paper is fragile and fiddly to work with. Be prepared to discard some rice papers if they tear and have extra rice papers in reserve to replace them.

Fresh herb and prawn rice paper rolls with peanut hoisin dipping sauce

The marriage of coriander and mint works beautifully with the tiger prawns in these simple rolls. You can make them three hours in advance.

QUICK & EASY

Makes 20

Ingredients

1 carrot, cut into julienne strips
1 tsp sugar
10 tiger prawns, cooked and peeled
5 small lettuce leaves
15g (½oz) coriander, separated into leaves
10 sheets of rice paper
20 mint leaves

For the sauce

2 tbsp hoisin sauce
2 tbsp smooth peanut butter
1 tbsp tomato ketchup
5 tbsp water

1 Combine the carrot strips with sugar and toss to coat each piece well. Let stand until wilted, 15 minutes.

2 Cut the prawns in half lengthways. Cut the lettuce leaves into 5cm x 2.5cm (2in x 1in) strips. Divide carrots and coriander into 20 equal-sized portions. Set aside.

3 Pour about 1.5cm (¾in) cold water into a shallow dish. Dip 1 sheet of rice paper into the water and leave to soften, 2 minutes. Remove and spread out on a dry tea towel. Cut in half.

4 Top 1 half sheet with 1 lettuce strip, 1 mint leaf, and 1 portion each of carrots and coriander. Roll rice paper over to enclose filling. Fold both ends of rice paper over the enclosed filling.

5 Place 1 prawn half, cut side down, on top. Continue rolling up into a cylinder and press the end with a wet finger to seal. Place the roll, seal side down, on a tray and cover with a dampened tea towel to keep moist. Repeat with the remaining half sheet rice paper, then start again with the remaining rice paper sheets and filling.

6 For the sauce, combine the hoisin, peanut butter, ketchup, and water. Serve rice paper rolls chilled or at room temperature with peanut hoisin dipping sauce.

GET AHEAD Prepare filling ingredients up to 1 day in advance. Cover and refrigerate. Make rolls up to 3 hours in advance. Cover with a dampened tea towel and refrigerate. Be sure to keep the tea towel moist.

Mini Peking duck pancakes with plum sauce

Taste these when you are assembling them to check that there is enough ginger, as it really brings out the flavour of the other ingredients.

Makes 20

Ingredients
1 tsp runny honey
1 tsp light soy sauce
1 duck breast, skinned
4cm (1½in) piece fresh ginger
2 spring onions
½ cucumber,
halved and seeded
20 long chives
10 ready-made
Chinese pancakes
2 tbsp plum sauce

1 Preheat oven to 200°C (400°F/Gas 6).

2 Combine the honey and soy. Brush the duck with the honey soy mixture. Roast duck until browned but still pink and juicy inside, 10 minutes. Cool. Slice duck breast diagonally into 0.5cm (¼in) thick slices.

3 Cut the ginger, spring onions, and cucumber into julienne strips.

4 Cut pancakes in half. Trim a 0.5cm (¼in) strip from the round edge of each pancake half to make 20 straight sided pieces. Spread ¼ tsp plum sauce in the centre of each piece. Divide duck slices and julienne strips among pancake strips. Roll up tightly and tie with a chive. Serve at room temperature.

GET AHEAD Roast duck breast up to 1 day in advance. Cover and refrigerate. Cut vegetables up to 1 day in advance. Store in an airtight container in the refrigerator. Slice duck and roll pancakes up to 1 hour in advance.

VARIATION Replace the duck with 250g (9oz) cooked pork fillet, thinly sliced. Replace the plum sauce with hoisin sauce and add 40 leaves of fresh mint, 2 leaves of mint in each roll.

Minted feta and pine nut filo rolls with lemon aïoli

These delicate little filo parcels are packed with the taste of summer. Keep any unused pieces of filo pastry covered, otherwise they will dry out.

Makes 20

Ingredients
100g (3½oz) pine nuts
100g (3½oz) feta cheese, crumbled
2 tbsp grated Parmesan cheese
2 tbsp finely chopped mint
grated zest of ½ lemon
1 tbsp lemon juice
¼ tsp freshly ground black pepper
30g (1oz) butter, melted
100g (3½oz) filo pastry
300ml (10fl oz) lemon aïoli (see p88)

1 Preheat oven to 180°C (350°F/Gas 4).

2 For the filling, toast the pine nuts in a dry pan over low heat until nutty and golden, 5 minutes. Cool. Place pine nuts, feta, Parmesan, mint, lemon zest, lemon juice, and pepper in a food processor; pulse until well blended.

3 Brush the butter on one side of 3 filo sheets and stack them together. If necessary, trim stacked filo sheets to measure 15cm (6in) in width.

4 Spread 2 tsp filling in a thin strip along the short end of the stacked filo. Roll the filo 1½ times around the filling. Brush with butter to seal.

5 Cut along the edge of the roll with a sharp knife to finish, then cut the finished roll in half. Place the 2 filo rolls seam-side down on a buttered baking sheet. Repeat the rolling process with the remaining filling and butter to make about 10 or 12 rolls per filo stack. Layer and butter a new stack of filo sheets when you no longer have room to start a new roll. Repeat buttering and layering with the remaining filo sheets, spreading and rolling with the remaining filling until you have run out of ingredients.

6 Brush filo rolls with butter. Bake until crisp and golden, 15 minutes. Cool on a wire rack. Serve warm or at room temperature, with lemon aïoli for dipping.

....

GET AHEAD Assemble up to 1 day in advance. Store covered in single layers not touching and refrigerate. Alternatively, assemble rolls and freeze up to 1 month in advance. Bake from frozen, 20–25 minutes.

Mini California rolls

A popular sushi dish, these rolls are great fun to make. To add variety, try using king prawns and lightly smoked salmon in the filling.

Makes 40

Ingredients
5 sheets of nori
300g (10oz) sushi rice
(see below)
½ cucumber, seeded and
cut into julienne strips
1 tsp wasabi
1 avocado, finely sliced
into 40 pieces
40 pickled ginger slices

Essential equipment
bamboo sushi mat

1 Fold the nori sheets into three, lengthways, to make a strip. Fold the strip into 3. Unfold and tear along the folded lines to make squares. Place the squares smooth side down.

2 Have a small bowl of water ready for moistening your fingers. Place 1 half, smooth side down, on the mat. Divide the rice and cucumber into 40 equal-sized portions. Moisten your fingers with water, then spread 1 rice portion in an even layer over the left half of 1 nori square.

3 Spread a thin line of wasabi lengthways along the centre of the rice with your finger. Arrange 1 portion cucumber, 1 avocado slice, and 1 ginger piece on top. Starting at the left corner, roll up the nori square like a cone, moistening with a wet finger to stick the nori together.

4 Repeat with remaining nori, rice, wasabi, cucumber, avocado, and ginger. Serve at room temperature.

GET AHEAD Assemble up to 1 hour in advance. Cover with cling film and store at room temperature.

SUSHI RICE

Makes 300g (10oz) | 175g (6oz) short-grained rice; 200ml (7fl oz) water; 125ml (4fl oz) rice vinegar; 5 tbsp sugar

Put rice in a large bowl. Cover with cold tap water and stir with your fingers until water turns cloudy. Pour off water. Repeat this until water is almost clear. Drain rice in a sieve. Put drained rice in a pan, add the water, cover, and bring to a boil over high heat. Boil for 2 minutes. Reduce heat to low and simmer until water is absorbed and rice is tender, 15 minutes. Remove from heat and let stand without lifting the lid, for 5 minutes. In separate pan, bring vinegar and sugar to a boil over medium heat, stirring until the sugar dissolves. Remove from heat and leave to cool. Turn the hot cooked rice out on to an oven tray and drizzle the vinegar and sugar mixture evenly on it. Toss the rice gently with a wooden spoon. Quickly cool the rice to room temperature by fanning it while continuing to toss. Cover the rice with a dampened tea towel and leave to cool.

GET AHEAD Make rice up to 3 hours in advance. Store covered with a dampened tea towel at room temperature.

COOK'S NOTE Fanning the rice as it cools will make the rice especially glossy. Use a piece of stiff cardboard or a baking sheet if you don't have a fan.

Cucumber nori sushi rolls

Crunchy cucumber with spicy wasabi are wrapped up in a sweet light sushi rice. You can find the ingredients in an Asian supermarket.

Makes 24

Ingredients
2 tsp sesame seeds
2 sheets of nori, halved
300g (10oz) sushi rice
(see opposite)
½ tsp wasabi paste
½ cucumber, seeded and
cut into julienne strips
2 tbsp pickled ginger
6 tbsp shoyu
(Japanese soy sauce)

Essential equipment
bamboo sushi mat

1 Toast the seeds in a dry pan over low heat until nutty and golden, 3 minutes. Cool.

2 Have a small bowl of water ready for moistening your fingers. Place 1 half piece nori, smooth side down, on the mat. Moisten your fingers with water, then spread a quarter of the rice in an even layer on the nori, leaving a 1cm (½in) strip uncovered at the end furthest away from you. Press down the rice with moistened fingers to pack firmly.

3 Spread a thin line of wasabi lengthways along the centre of the rice with your finger. Arrange a quarter of the cucumber, sesame seeds, and ginger on top, making sure the fillings extend completely to each end of the rice.

4 Pick up the bamboo mat and tightly roll rice around the filling, pulling the mat as you roll. Unroll mat. Repeat with remaining nori, rice, wasabi, cucumber, sesame seeds, and ginger.

5 Cut each nori roll into 6 equal-sized pieces with a moist knife. Serve chilled or at room temperature with shoyu for dipping.

....

GET AHEAD Make, but do not cut, nori rolls up to 1 day in advance. Store wrapped in cling film at room temperature.

Sesame sushi rolls

Colourful and nutty, these little sushi rolls have contrasting textures, which make them so appealing to eat.

Makes 24

Ingredients

3 tbsp sesame seeds
125g (4½oz) medium prawns
2 sheets of nori, halved
300g (10oz) sushi rice (see p194)
½ tsp wasabi paste
½ cucumber, seeded and cut into julienne strips
6 tbsp shoyu (Japanese soy sauce)

Essential equipment

bamboo sushi mat

1 Toast the sesame seeds in a dry pan over low heat until nutty and golden, 3 minutes. Cool. Cut the prawns in half lengthways. Have a small bowl of water ready for moistening your fingers.

2 Cut 1 sheet of cling film just larger than 1 nori half. Place 1 nori half, smooth side down, on the mat. Moisten your fingers with water, then spread a quarter of the rice in an even layer on the nori. Cover with the cling film.

3 Pick up the nori, carefully turn over, and place on the mat, cling film side down. The nori should now be facing up. Spread a thin line of wasabi lengthways along the centre of the nori with your fingers.

4 Arrange a quarter of the prawns, cucumber, and 1 tsp sesame seeds on top, making sure the fillings extend completely to each end. Pick up the bamboo mat and cling film and tightly roll rice around filling, pressing down firmly as you roll. Unroll the mat and cling film.

5 Gently roll the rice roll in half of the remaining sesame seeds. Roll up tightly in cling film, twisting the ends to secure. Repeat with remaining nori, rice, wasabi, prawns, cucumber, and sesame seeds.

6 Trim the ends of each roll to neaten, then cut each rice roll into 6 equal-sized pieces with a moist knife. Remove cling film from the cut pieces. Serve at room temperature with shoyu for dipping.

···

GET AHEAD Assemble, but do not cut, the rice rolls up to 1 day in advance. Store wrapped in cling film at room temperature. Cut when ready to serve.

COOK'S NOTE We used a mixture of black and brown sesame seeds for coating the roll that is pictured here. Black sesame seeds are available to buy in specialist stores. For an alternative coating, try 2 tbsp red lumpfish roe.

Spinach, smoked trout, and herbed cream roulade

To add variety, use smoked salmon slices instead of trout. Make sure that the wilted spinach is dry, otherwise it will make the filling watery.

Makes 30

Ingredients

For the roulade
350g (12oz) spinach
3 eggs, separated
¼ tsp ground nutmeg
1 tsp salt and ½ tsp freshly ground black pepper

For the filling
200g (7oz) cream cheese
2 tbsp finely chopped fresh dill
grated zest and juice of 1 lemon
salt and freshly ground black pepper
200g (7oz) smoked trout slices

Essential equipment
35cm x 25cm (14in x 10in) Swiss roll tray lined with buttered baking parchment

1 Preheat oven to 200°C (400°F/Gas 6).

2 Bring a pan of water to a boil and add spinach. When the water returns to a boil, drain and refresh the spinach in cold water. Squeeze spinach dry with hands.

3 Place the spinach, egg yolks, nutmeg, and salt and pepper in a food processor or blender; pulse to a smooth purée.

4 Whisk the egg whites until they hold soft peaks. Fold egg whites lightly into the spinach until evenly combined. Spread the spinach mixture into the prepared tray.

5 Bake until set, 10–12 minutes. Turn baked roulade out on to a sheet of baking parchment. Leave to cool.

6 For the filling, combine the cream cheese, dill, lemon zest and juice. Add salt and pepper to taste.

7 Turn out the roulade and peel off the baking parchment. Cut roulade in half widthways. Place each half on a piece of cling film. Spread filling evenly over both roulade halves, to within about 1cm (½in) of the edges. Cover each with a layer of trout slices. Sprinkle with pepper.

8 Roll up each roulade half from the long edge. Wrap in cling film, twisting the ends to secure.

9 Refrigerate rolls for 1 hour. With a serrated knife, trim ends of both roulades. Cut each roulade into 10 slices. Discard cling film after slicing. Serve chilled or at room temperature.

GET AHEAD Make roulade up to 1 day in advance. Refrigerate. Slice up to 1 hour before serving.

Rolled parsley frittatine with black olive ricotta

A vegetarian treat, this wonderful canapé will be popular with all your guests. You can make the frittatine a day in advance.

Makes 20

Ingredients

For the frittatine
3 eggs, beaten
3 tbsp double cream
1 tbsp melted butter
1 tbsp finely chopped parsley
⅛ tsp ground nutmeg
½ tsp salt and ¼ tsp freshly ground black pepper
1 tsp butter for pan

For the filling
125g (4½ oz) ricotta cheese
150g (5½ oz) pitted black olives, finely chopped
salt and freshly ground black pepper

Essential equipment
24cm (9½in) non-stick or heavy frying pan

1 Beat the eggs, cream, butter, parsley, nutmeg, and salt and pepper until combined.

2 Melt 1 tsp butter in a pan over medium heat. Pour in half of the egg mixture. Cook until golden and set on both sides, 5 minutes in total.

3 Slide frittatine from pan on to kitchen paper to drain. Repeat with remaining butter and egg mixture. Leave to cool.

4 For the filling, combine the ricotta and olives. Add salt and pepper to taste. Spread each cooled frittatina evenly with half of the filling to within 1cm (½in) of edges. Roll up separately.

5 Wrap each in cling film, twisting the ends to secure. Refrigerate for 1 hour. With a serrated knife, trim ends of both frittatina.

6 Cut each frittatina into 10 slices. Discard the cling film after slicing. Serve chilled or at room temperature.

GET AHEAD Make frittatine up to 1 day in advance. Refrigerate. Slice up to 1 hour before serving.

Egg, caper, and cress finger sandwiches

Capers season these afternoon tea sandwiches beautifully. Traditionally, egg sandwiches are served on white bread, but wholemeal also works well.

Makes 30

Ingredients
4 medium eggs
1 tbsp finely chopped drained capers
15g (½oz) watercress, finely chopped
4 tbsp mayonnaise (see p88)
salt and freshly ground black pepper
45g (1½oz) butter, softened
10 medium slices white bread

1 Place the eggs in a pan of cold water. Bring water to a boil, then reduce heat and simmer for 8 minutes. Drain and cool eggs completely in cold water.

2 Shell and chop eggs. Combine eggs, capers, watercress, and mayonnaise. Add salt and pepper to taste. Spread the butter, then egg, and mayonnaise evenly over 5 bread slices.

3 Top with remaining bread. Cut off crusts using a serrated knife and discard. Cut each sandwich in half, then cut each half into 3 fingers about 3.5cm (1½in) wide. Serve chilled or at room temperature.

....

GET AHEAD Make sandwiches up to 1 day in advance, but do not remove crusts or cut. Cover with cling film and refrigerate. Cut sandwiches up to 3 hours in advance.

Mini croque monsieur

Make batches of these warm crisp sandwiches, as one plate will not go very far. Prepare the sandwiches one day ahead and bake just before serving.

Makes 20

Ingredients
10 medium white
bread slices
85g (3oz) soft butter
4 tsp Dijon mustard
5 ham slices
200g (7oz) Gruyère
cheese, grated

1 Preheat oven to 200°C (400°F/Gas 6).

2 Spread the butter onto both sides of each slice of bread. Spread mustard onto one side of bread.

3 Top 5 bread slices with one slice ham each. Sprinkle half the cheese over the 5 slices. Press the remaining bread slices on top to make sandwiches. Place on a baking sheet.

4 Sprinkle the remaining cheese across the top of the sandwiches. Bake until cheese is golden and melted, 10 minutes. Cool slightly. Cut off the crusts with a serrated knife. Cut each sandwich into 4 squares. Serve warm.

....

GET AHEAD Assemble sandwiches up to 1 day in advance. Cover and refrigerate. Bake just before serving.

COOK'S NOTE When making the mini croque madame variation, use the tip of a small sharp knife to crack open the quail eggs.

VARIATION
Mini croque madame Use 100g (3½oz) Gruyère cheese instead of 200g (7oz). Fill sandwiches as directed, but do not top with cheese. Bake until bread is toasted, 10 minutes. Cut sandwiches as directed. Fry 20 quail eggs in 30g (1oz) butter. Top each sandwich square with a quail egg. Sprinkle over salt and pepper and serve immediately.

Mozzarella, basil, and sun-dried tomato croque monsieur Replace the ham with 10 sun-dried tomatoes, drained, patted dry, and thinly sliced, top with 10 large basil leaves and 140g (5oz) sliced mozzarella. Garnish with capers.

6 ways with **finger sandwiches**

Make little finger sandwiches with these classic and delicious fillings, or try your own favourite flavours and ingredients. These recipes make 24 mini sandwiches.

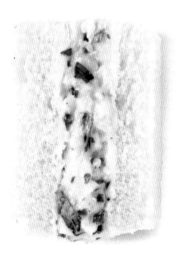

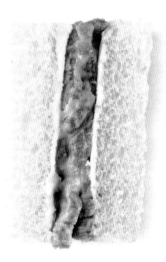

chicken and tarragon

Spread 8 slices of medium sliced bread with softened butter. Mix 200g (7oz) shredded cooked chicken breast with 3 tbsp mayonnaise, 1½ tbsp wholegrain mustard, 1 tbsp finely chopped tarragon, and salt and black pepper. Spread the chicken mixture on 4 of the slices and top with the remaining 4 slices. Cut off the crusts using a serrated knife and discard. Cut the sandwiches into 6 mini sandwiches to serve.

prawn, avocado, and bacon

Spread 8 slices of medium sliced granary bread with softened butter. Mix 1 diced ripe avocado with 1 tbsp lemon juice, salt and black pepper, 3 tbsp mayonnaise (see p88), 200g (7oz) small prawns, and 100g (3½oz) cooked diced bacon. Spread the mixture evenly over 4 slices of bread and top with the remaining 4 slices. Cut off the crusts using a serrated knife and discard. Cut into 6 mini sandwiches to serve.

rare roast beef and horseradish cream

Spread 8 slices of medium sliced bread and spread with softened butter. Mix 2 tbsp mayonnaise (see p88), 1 tbsp Dijon mustard, and 1 tbsp horseradish cream. Spread 4 slices of bread with horseradish cream and top with 150g (5oz) thinly sliced (fat removed) rare roast beef. Top with the remaining 4 slices. Cut off the crusts and discard. Cut into 6 mini sandwiches to serve.

Know-how... making finger sandwiches

GET AHEAD You can make these mini finger sandwiches the day before if you store them in an airtight container in between sheets of very slightly damp greaseproof paper. However, do not remove the crusts or cut them until the next day otherwise they may go soggy.

COOK'S NOTE Slice the sandwiches into fingers 1 hour before serving, and keep them covered until serving. You can vary the bread, but soft bread will be easier to cut and eat. Make sure that the butter is softened, as this makes it easier to spread it over the bread.

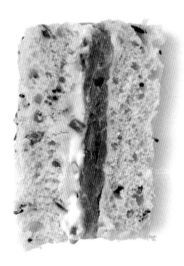

crab and watercress mayonnaise

Spread 8 slices of medium sliced wholemeal bread with softened butter. Combine 150g (5oz) crabmeat with 3 tbsp mayonnaise (see p88), 1 bunch watercress, stalks removed and finely chopped, salt and pepper, 1 tbsp lemon juice, 1 tbsp grated lemon zest, and a pinch of cayenne. Spread evenly over 4 slices of bread and top with the remaining 4 slices. Cut off the crusts and discard. Cut into 6 sandwiches to serve.

cucumber and mint

Spread 8 slices of medium sliced white bread with softened butter. Thinly slice 1 cucumber, place in a colander, and lightly scatter over sea salt, then leave for 2 hours. Gently pat off the salt and pat dry with kitchen paper. Evenly distribute the cucumber over 4 slices and scatter over 20 mint leaves and black pepper. Top with the remaining 4 slices. Cut off the crusts using a serrated knife and discard. Cut into 6 mini sandwiches to serve.

smoked salmon and citrus-chive cream

Spread 8 slices of seeded medium sliced bread with softened butter. Mix 175g (6oz) cream cheese with 1 tbsp lemon zest, black pepper, a pinch of salt, a pinch of cayenne pepper, and 15g (½oz) chives, finely chopped. Spread the mixture evenly over 4 slices of bread and top with 200g (7oz) smoked salmon. Top with the remaining 4 slices. Cut off the crusts using a serrated knife and discard. Cut into 6 mini sandwiches to serve.

Rosemary mini muffins with smoked ham and peach relish

Make the mini muffins ahead of time then fill with the best-quality smoked ham and peach salsa, or choose another favourite fruity chutney.

Makes 20

Ingredients

For the mini muffins
175g (6oz) plain flour
1 tsp baking powder
1 tsp baking soda
¼ tsp salt
2 tsp finely chopped rosemary
6 tbsp caster sugar
1 egg, beaten
125ml (4fl oz) milk
3 tbsp melted butter

For the filling
1 peach, fresh or tinned
1 tsp cider vinegar
4 tbsp cream cheese
150g (5½oz) smoked ham slices

Essential equipment
2 mini muffin tins
(12 cup), buttered

1 For the muffins, preheat oven to 200°C (400°F/Gas 6).

2 Sift the flour, baking powder, baking soda, salt, and rosemary into a bowl. Make a well in the centre. Add remaining ingredients. Gently fold everything together to make a wet batter.

3 Spoon batter into 20 of the buttered muffin cups. Bake until golden brown and firm to the touch, 12 minutes. Turn out and cool completely on a wire rack.

4 For the relish, finely dice the peach. Toss with vinegar. Cut muffins in half. Spread each bottom half with cream cheese.

5 Cut ham slices into 20 wide strips (2.5cm/1in). Place 1 ham strip on to each muffin.

6 Spoon the peach relish on top. Cover with top half of muffin. Serve at room temperature.

....

GET AHEAD Bake muffins up to 1 day in advance. Store in an airtight container. Fill muffins up to 2 hours before serving. Store at room temperature.

COOK'S NOTE These mini muffins are delicious enough to be served without a filling. Place in a preheated 180°C (350°F/Gas 4) oven for 5 minutes before serving.

VARIATION Try the combination of smoked duck and redcurrant jelly as an alternative filling for these flavourful rosemary mini muffins.

Baby bagels with cream cheese, salmon, and dill

Try sprinkling grated lemon zest on top of the salmon before adding the bagel top to finish off these satisfying and delicious little mouthfuls.

Makes 20

Ingredients

For the baby bagels
1 recipe unbaked bread dough (see pp134–5)
1 egg yolk beaten with 1 tbsp water
2 tbsp poppy or sesame seeds

For the filling
125g (4½oz) cream cheese
200g (7oz) smoked salmon
20 dill sprigs
freshly ground black pepper

Essential equipment
slotted spoon

1 Preheat oven to 200°C (400°F/Gas 6).

2 For the baby bagels, divide the dough into 20 walnut-sized pieces. Shape each piece into a ball. Form each ball into a ring by inserting a floured finger into the centre. Work your finger in a circle to widen the hole.

3 Bring a pan of water to a boil over high heat, then reduce heat to simmering. Working in batches, use the slotted spoon to lower bagels into the water. Boil until bagels rise to surface.

4 Remove from water to an oiled baking sheet with the slotted spoon. Repeat with remaining bagels. Brush bagels with beaten egg and sprinkle with seeds. Bake until golden, 10 minutes.

5 Slice bagels in half and toast lightly. Spread bottom halves with cream cheese.

6 Top with salmon and dill and sprinkle with pepper. Cover with top halves. Serve at room temperature.

....

GET AHEAD Bake bagels up to 3 days in advance. Store in an airtight container. Freeze bagels up to 1 month in advance. Fill bagels up to 5 hours in advance. Cover and store at room temperature.

sweet bites

Triple chocolate biscottini with hazelnuts

These chocolate biscottini can be made well in advance. Package any leftovers and give as a party gift to your guests.

Makes 50

Ingredients
200g (7oz) plain flour
60g (2oz) cocoa powder
¾ tsp baking powder
¼ tsp salt
150g (5½oz) caster sugar
60g (2oz) dark chocolate, chopped
3 eggs, beaten
1 tsp vanilla extract
100g (3½oz) hazelnuts, skinned
100g (3½oz) white chocolate to decorate

Essential equipment
paper piping bag

1 Preheat oven to 180°C (350°F/Gas 4).

2 Sift the flour, cocoa, baking powder, and salt into a bowl. Add the sugar, dark chocolate, eggs, and vanilla and mix with a fork to form a rough dough. Alternatively, place flour, cocoa, baking powder, salt, sugar, chocolate, eggs, and vanilla in a food processor; pulse to form a rough dough.

3 Knead the hazelnuts into the dough with your hands. Divide dough into 4 equal-sized pieces. Shape each piece into logs, 2.5cm (1in) thick and 30cm (12in) long. Place logs on floured baking sheets and bake until firm to the touch, 25 minutes. Remove and leave until cool enough to handle.

4 With a serrated knife, cut each biscotti log on the diagonal into thick slices (1cm/½in). Place the slices in a single layer on baking sheets. Bake until crisp and dry, 15 minutes. Cool on a wire rack. Melt the white chocolate. Fill the piping bag with chocolate. Drizzle over the biscottini.

GET AHEAD Make up to 2 weeks in advance. Store in an airtight container at room temperature. Alternatively, freeze the unbaked biscotti logs up to 1 month in advance. Defrost overnight in the refrigerator before baking.

COOK'S NOTE For an alternative finish, try dipping one end of each biscottini into the melted white chocolate.

Strawberry and pistachio mini meringues

Crisp, nutty, chewy textured mini meringues are perfect to serve at a summer get-together. Use whole raspberries instead of strawberries.

Makes 20

Ingredients
5 strawberries
75ml (2½fl oz) whipping cream
1 tbsp caster sugar
300ml (10fl oz) baked pistachio mini meringues
2 tsp icing sugar for dusting
2 tbsp chopped pistachios

1 Cut the strawberries into quarters.

2 Whip the cream until it holds soft peaks. Whisk in 1 tbsp caster sugar.

3 Top each meringue with 1 tsp cream and dust with icing sugar. Arrange strawberry quarters on top. Garnish with chopped pistachios.

....

GET AHEAD Assemble meringues 3 hours before serving; keep at room temperature.

VANILLA MINI MERINGUES

Makes 20 | 2 egg whites at room temperature; 125g (4½oz) caster sugar; ½ tsp vanilla extract

Put the egg whites in a large, clean bowl and whisk until the meringue holds soft peaks. Add the sugar, 1 tbsp at a time, whisking well after each addition. Continue whisking until the whites are stiff and glossy. Fold in the vanilla with a rubber spatula and any additional flavouring, if using, according to the instructions given for the flavour variations.

Preheat oven to 180°C (350°F/Gas 4). Use the tip of two teaspoons to place small walnut-sized spoonfuls of meringue, 2.5cm (1in) apart, on to baking parchment-lined baking sheets. Make an indent in the centre of each mini meringue with the back of one teaspoon. Bake for 5 minutes, then turn the oven temperature down to 120°C (250°F/Gas ½). Continue baking until firm to the touch, 20 minutes.

Leave to cool completely before removing the mini meringues from the baking sheet.

GET AHEAD Bake up to 2 days in advance. Store in an airtight container at room temperature.

COOK'S NOTE Make sure the bowl is grease-free or your whites will not stiffen. If in doubt, wipe with kitchen paper dipped in vinegar before you begin. A daring but effective way to check if the whites are stiff is to hold the bowl upside down: the meringue should not fall out!

VARIATION Add the flavouring to the meringue with the vanilla. Fold in with a spatula with the vanilla until evenly combined.
Chocolate meringue Fold in 1 tsp sifted cocoa powder.
Hazelnut meringue Fold in 2 tbsp ground hazelnuts.
Muscovado meringue Fold in 1 tbsp dark brown sugar.
Pistachio meringue Fold in 1 tbsp chopped unsalted pistachios.

Muscovado and fig mini meringues

Muscovado sugar is used to sweeten these little meringues and give them a toffee-like flavour. They will be popular with everyone.

Makes 20

Ingredients
2 figs
300ml (10fl oz) baked muscovado mini meringues (see opposite)
125ml (4fl oz) crème fraîche
2 tsp cocoa powder for dusting
60g (2oz) plain chocolate, melted

1 Cut the figs in half, then slice each half into 5 slivers.

2 Top individual meringues with 1 tsp crème fraîche and dust lightly with cocoa powder.

3 Arrange 1 fig sliver on top then, using a teaspoon, drizzle with melted chocolate. Serve at room temperature.

GET AHEAD Assemble meringues up to 3 hours in advance; keep at room temperature.

Cherry and almond frangipane tartlets

A French classic, almonds also go well with many fruits such as raspberries, blackberries, and apricots.

Makes 20

Ingredients
30g (1oz) butter, softened
2 tbsp caster sugar
30g (1oz) ground almonds
1 egg yolk
1 tbsp double cream
20 baked pastry tartlets
(see pp172–3)
20 cherries
(about 175g/6oz, stoned)
2 tsp icing sugar for dusting

1 Preheat oven to 180°C (350°F/Gas 4).

2 Combine the butter, sugar, almonds, egg yolk, and cream until well blended. Divide evenly among tartlets.

3 Place 1 cherry on top of each tartlet. Bake until set and golden, 15 minutes. Cool completely. Dust with icing sugar to garnish. Serve at room temperature.

....

GET AHEAD Bake filled tartlets up to 1 day in advance. Store in an airtight container at room temperature. Garnish just before serving.

COOK'S NOTE Use tinned black or morello cherries when fresh cherries are out of season.

Caramelized lemon tartlets

To add variety, try this recipe with lime instead of lemon, and serve with a spoonful of whipped double cream.

Makes 20

Ingredients
1 egg, beaten
2 tbsp caster sugar
2 tbsp lemon juice
grated zest of 1 lemon
2 tbsp double cream
20 baked pastry tartlets
(see pp172–3)
2 tbsp caster sugar
to caramelize

1 Preheat oven to 190°C (375°F/Gas 5).

2 Whisk the egg and sugar together until sugar dissolves. Whisk in the lemon juice, zest, and cream until just combined. Leave for 5 minutes. Skim any froth off the top.

3 Pour lemon mixture into baked tartlets. Bake until only just set, 5–8 minutes. Cool to room temperature.

4 Preheat the grill. Sprinkle tartlets with a thin layer of sugar. Place tartlets under the grill as close to the element as possible until the sugar has coloured, 1–2 minutes. Watch constantly to avoid burning. Alternatively, use a cook's blow torch. Serve at room temperature.

GET AHEAD Bake filled tartlets up to 1 day in advance. Cover and refrigerate. Caramelize tops up to 3 hours before serving.

Tiny Devonshire cream tea scones with raspberry conserve

Delightful afternoon tea fare, everyone will adore these little scones. Try experimenting with heart-shaped cookie cutters.

Makes 20

Ingredients
175g (6oz) plain flour
1½ tsp baking powder
pinch of salt
45g (1½oz) butter, diced
1½ tbsp caster sugar
1 egg, beaten
60ml (2fl oz) cream
125ml (4fl oz) raspberry conserve
125ml (4fl oz) double cream

Essential equipment
4cm (1½in) fluted cookie cutter

1 Preheat oven to 200°C (400°F/Gas 6).

2 Sift the flour, baking powder, and salt. Crumble the butter into the flour with your fingers until the mixture resembles fine crumbs. Stir in the sugar (omit if making savoury scones) and any additional flavouring, if using.

3 With a fork, stir in the egg and enough cream to make a soft dough. Turn the dough on to a floured surface and knead lightly until smooth. Gently roll out to a 2.5cm (1in) thickness and stamp out 10 rounds with the cookie cutter.

4 Place the rounds on a greased and floured baking sheet. Bake until firm and golden, 8–10 minutes. Cool on a wire rack.

5 Cut each scone in half. Whip the double cream until it holds soft peaks.

6 Top each scone half with 1 tsp each conserve and cream. Serve at room temperature.

GET AHEAD Bake the scones up to 1 week ahead. Store in an airtight container at room temperature. Top up to 30 minutes in advance.

COOK'S NOTE Cover the scones with a cloth as they cool. This will keep some of the steam in, making the scones soft, moist, and light.

VARIATION
Tiny dill scones Replace the sugar with 1 tbsp finely chopped dill.

Mini chocolate truffle cakes

My advice is to double the recipe. Make these decadent cakes five days ahead and then just slice or cut into shape a few hours before serving.

Makes 20

Ingredients

For the cake
150g (5½oz) butter
400g (14oz) dark chocolate, broken into pieces
150g (5½oz) granulated sugar
5 eggs, separated
45g (1½oz) flour

For the glaze
5 tbsp double cream
75g (2½oz) dark chocolate, broken into pieces

Essential equipment
35cm x 25cm (14in x 10in) Swiss roll tray lined with buttered baking parchment
4.25cm (1¾in) cookie cutter

1 Preheat oven to 150°C (300°F/Gas 2).

2 For the cake, melt the butter and chocolate together in a double boiler over low heat. Stir continuously until smooth and melted. Remove from heat and cool to tepid.

3 Beat sugar, egg yolks, and flour into the cool chocolate. Whisk egg whites until they hold soft peaks.

4 Gently fold chocolate mixture into egg whites until evenly combined. Pour batter into the lined tray. Bake until firm to the touch, 20 minutes. Cool completely.

5 For the glaze, heat the cream in a pan just below the boiling point. Remove from heat. Stir in chocolate until melted and smooth. Cool until slightly thickened, 30 minutes.

6 Stamp cooled cake into 25 rounds with the cookie cutter. Spoon 1 heaped tsp of the glaze over each cake round. Serve at room temperature.

....

GET AHEAD Bake cake up to 5 days in advance. Store at room temperature. Alternatively, bake and freeze cake up to 1 month in advance. Defrost in refrigerator overnight. Cut and glaze cake rounds up to 3 hours in advance. Leave at room temperature, until ready to serve.

COOK'S NOTE A double boiler is a set of two pans stacked on top of each other and is used as a bain-marie or water bath on the stove. It is ideal for melting chocolate.

Mini sticky orange and almond cakes

These wheat-free cakes, flavoured with whole oranges, are wonderful served with Greek yogurt or crème fraîche. They keep very well.

Makes 25

Ingredients
2 whole oranges, unpeeled
6 eggs, beaten
250g (9oz) granulated sugar
250g (9oz) ground almonds
1 tsp baking powder
4 tbsp pomegranate kernels
to decorate
150ml (5fl oz) Greek-style yogurt

Essential equipment
35cm x 25cm (14in x 10in) Swiss roll tray lined with buttered baking parchment
4.25cm (1¾ in) cookie cutter

1 Cook whole oranges in boiling water until soft, 1½ hours. Cool completely. Preheat oven to 190°C (375°F/Gas 5).

2 For the cake, cut oranges in half and remove any pips. Place in a food processor; process to a smooth purée.

3 Add the eggs, sugar, almonds, and baking powder; pulse until well combined. Pour batter into the lined tray. Bake until firm to the touch, 40 minutes. Cool completely.

4 Cut the pomegranate in half through the middle of the stem end. Cut each half into quarters. Pull stem ends of each quarter towards each other, bending peel back to release pomegranate kernels.

5 Stamp cake into 20 rounds with the cookie cutter. Spoon ½ tsp yogurt on to each cake round. Decorate with pomegranate kernels. Serve at room temperature.

GET AHEAD Make cake up to 2 days in advance. Store at room temperature. Alternatively, bake and freeze cake up to 1 month in advance. Defrost in the refrigerator overnight. Decorate cakes up to 3 hours ahead. Leave at room temperature, until ready to serve.

Acknowledgments

With huge thanks to my gorgeous family, friends, colleagues, and clients – may the party continue!
Victoria Blashford-Snell

Dorling Kindersley would like to thank the following:

Jane Bamforth for recipe testing; Janet Shuter for indexing; Claire Cross for proofreading; Iska Lupton and Chris Mooney for editorial assistance; Chhaya Sajwan for design assistance; William Reavell for photography; Katherine Mead for photography art direction, Jane Lawrie for food styling, Paul Jackman and Iska Lupton for food styling assistance, Joanne Harris for props styling; Ian O'Leary for original photography; and Eric Treuille for original food styling.

About the authors

Victoria Blashford-Snell first began cooking in pubs and restaurants in the UK. As a result of her zest for travel, she developed an imaginative variety of tastes, from the Mediterranean to the Great Barrier Reef to the Himalayas. Today she runs a successful catering business and teaches regular cookery courses in the UK.

Victoria has written several popular cookbooks including *Diva Cooking* and *The Cooking Book* (DK), and has co-authored six Books for Cooks titles. She regularly appears on food shows in the US and Canada.

Eric Treuille has been passionate about food since he worked as a *mitron* (baby baker) in his uncle's boulangerie in France. He has cooked professionally in Paris, London, and New York, until work as a stylist with Anne Willan and Le Cordon Bleu introduced him to the world of cookbooks. Currently director of Books for Cooks, the internationally famous bookshop and cooking school in London, Eric is also the author of *Barbecue, Bread, Pasta, The Organic Cookbook*, and *Le Cordon Bleu's Complete Guide to Cooking Techniques*.